MW00976966

Elaine Long

GOD SENDS THE WORDS
I ONLY HOLD THE PEN

Thoughts from the heart

ELAINE LONG

authorHOUSE®

AuthorHouse™
1663 Liberty Drive
Bloomington, IN 47403
www.authorhouse.com
Phone: 1-800-839-8640

© 2012 by Elaine Long. All rights reserved.

No part of this book may be reproduced, stored in a retrieval system, or transmitted by any means without the written permission of the author.

Published by AuthorHouse   03/23/2012

ISBN: 978-1-4685-6021-3 (sc)
ISBN: 978-1-4685-6020-6 (hc)
ISBN: 978-1-4685-6019-0 (e)

Library of Congress Control Number: 2012904459

This book is printed on acid-free paper.

Because of the dynamic nature of the Internet, any web addresses or links contained in this book may have changed since publication and may no longer be valid. The views expressed in this work are solely those of the author and do not necessarily reflect the views of the publisher, and the publisher hereby disclaims any responsibility for them.

CONTENTS

GOD SENDS THE WORDS

PRAYER AND FAITH: NOTHING IS BEYOND HIS REACH

God and God's Blessings

Heaven: Our Eternal Home

Family, Values and Teachings

FRIENDS: GOD'S GIFTS

TEARS OF GRIEF

HOLIDAYS AND SEASONS

GROWING OLD AND LIFE'S SURPRISES

LESSONS LEARNED

PARADISE IS AT THE BEACH

MY LEGACY IS THE VALUE OF MY YEARS

Dedication Page

To family and friends here and those who call Heaven home. Without their encouragement, patience, and love this book would not have been compiled, and most of all to God, for He sent the words.

ACKNOWLEDGEMENTS

My gratitude is to more people than I can name. Their inspiration, wisdom, support, guidance and faith in me have made this adventure possible and especially to the beach girls who have given more than they received.

LIGHTHOUSE LAMP

September's harvest moon is awesome to view over land.
However a chance to see a full moon over water is grand.
It was a spectacular view at the beach on that clear night.
The photographer captured the moon as a lighthouse light.

There was much thought and design into this camera shot.
She did so much measuring and planning for the right spot.
The welcoming glow from the lighthouse lamp is the moon.
Another chance for this amazing picture won't be soon.

Debra Stephens 9/2011

GOD SENDS THE WORDS

AN ENORMOUS TRUST

If there are rhymes or reasons to poems that I write.
It has to be from an idea God put in my heart at night.
Verses at least most of the time from my pen will flow.
Long before the thought appears for my mind to know.

I've said I do not take any credit for where the poems led.
I simply hold the pen that writes the words God has said.
An idea or thought slowly occurs on the page appearing.
It comes from the words upon my heart I keep hearing.

The thought will normally flow at a steady, constant pace.
Until I ponder and mull over a final line all over the place.
As I seek the remarks to give the intended point or view.
God completes it with the right words for hope to renew.

I am constantly amazed at the deep thoughts He inspires.
Only He can supply everything our heart needs or desires.
An enormous trust has been simply loaned to my heart.
The words being written on the paper is the easiest part.

The vast depth of the love of God cannot be measured.
The important thing is that it can forever be treasured.
When His lines unfold upon the page, it is nothing I do.
Lord, with reverence, respect and awe I say, thank you.

I Only Know

Sometimes the words are slow, yet other times they tumble and flow.
I have no idea where they come from or a single clue why they go.
At times a thought or an unforgettable memory across my mind leaps.
Other times, it is from a recollection left deep in my heart for keeps.

Sometimes it is the remembrance of a painful reflection of the past.
Part of the time it comes from a soothing thought of peace at last.
There are times a word or just a line stands out in something said.
At times a simple phrase comes to mind long after I have gone to bed.

A few times the words were on the tip of my tongue to another to say.
In the sincere hope it might lighten a load or brighten someone's day.
Nevertheless, most of the time it is for me and trying to ease my soul.
Else, all of the words running around in my heart will make me so old.

If it puts some thoughts into words someone can see and understand.
Then they are welcome to draw any and all the reassurance they can.
I never know if it will be comforting to some other hearts on the mend.
I only know God gives the words for my poems, I simply hold the pen.

LIFE IS ALWAYS A CHALLENGE

Poems are writings from thoughts lying on my heart.
At the time they were penned they played a large part.
Sometimes only the concept is implied from my mind.
A true concern may be found sitting between the lines.

By removing or repairing some feelings of every kind.
Words allow peace and an outlet for a troubled mind.
If my process of expression permits you some hope.
Feel free to use my thoughts if they help you to cope.

It is terribly hard to hide an aching heart behind a smile.
Or to control the tears that are company on every mile.
Regret should not be a burden for the shoulder to hold.
It is simply too much baggage to assume the guilt role.

Life is always a challenge and it is not always very fair.
One can aim to do their best when troubles come to bear.
Moving forward and trying not to look backward anymore.
Taking each day as it comes with whatever may be in store.

One must live each day as if it were the last on earth to see.
Enjoying all the beauty placed in each day for you and me.
My path was not of my plans; it was and is of God's way.
He had a solution in mind before I had a problem any day.

HE IS THERE

Life experiences for one often allow another some aid.
If another needs comfort then the debt has been paid.
As with the creation of the universe God is in control.
No matter how rough the road this fact never gets old.

He uses others to be a comfort when anyone has a need.
Only God will send what is helpful for others to receive.
Sometimes the words of help are given by Him in a verse.
Words often soothe or prevent nerves from getting worse.

A gift of words from God can come in a poem or a rhyme.
It may offer comfort and joy and peace at the proper time.
The words come from the pen in a tumbling or gentle flow.
A quill holder is only His messenger to whomever they go.

Other's words are not the only way God touches the heart.
He speaks softly to all of us and we hear if we do our part.
Sometimes life's noises prevent us from hearing His voice.
Other times we don't listen and that is each one's choice.

This is a most comforting thought which gets us through.
Trust in God to walk and talk with us in all we have to do.
He is there but maybe wary enough to wait until one asks.
Talk to Him and whatever lies ahead will be a small task.

Elaine Long

TAKE MY WORDS LIGHTLY

Now and then something odd crosses my mind.
It comes from deep within this old soul of mine.
As if on a mission the words upon the paper leap.
Hidden and confined thoughts I can no longer keep.

Tumbling out from down deep inside before I know.
Sometimes slowly but sometimes the words just flow.
I make a feeble attempt at any rhythm or simple rhyme.
It has not a reason or a subject until I hear the first line.

Most of the writings are about circumstances of my heart.
So it begins like an emotional wave right from the start.
The feelings are of sadness or joy or love and some pain.
I never know what idea will keep me awake once again.

A word can or a phrase or possibly some passing thought.
All I can imagine is a gift from God to my heart taught.
For it certainly isn't any talent I have on my very own.
This need to write it down came only since I stand alone.

Any benefit from my jumble of words may be only for me.
On paper the anguish deep from within my heart I can see.
Could this way of venting allow me to go one more mile?
If so then maybe one day my heart can once again smile.

You just take my words lightly and only upon your sleeve.
Don't take them to heart and cry or ever once even believe.
I did not mean to make you sad by reading all of my phrases.
Or to cause anyone pain from perusing these misery phases.

Read them quickly and softly or even laugh heartily out loud.
Make such a noise that you likely will draw a puzzled crowd.
For laughter will remove some of your stress and life's pain.
If my words offer any comfort then my time was not in vain.

Elaine Long

PRAYER AND FAITH:

NOTHING IS BEYOND HIS REACH

MY PRAYER

Lord, thank you for family and friends I hold so dear.
May each one in my heart and mind always stay near.
Please bless and comfort them each and every day.
Keep them all safe and watch over them this I pray.

When the night is over and tomorrow is another day.
Let their cares and worries all be brushed far away.
Guide their paths with much wisdom along their way.
Remind them the troubles on you they can always lay.

Lord please protect and give strength to one and all.
I pray you never let them even stumble much less fall.
Let them know that with you they have nothing to fear.
May they never forget Lord I hold them so very near.

LORD, I DON'T KNOW . . . .

Lord, I just don't know where I'm walking,
I just know you are walking with me.
Lord, I don't feel any joy or hope sometimes,
I just know my strength comes from thee.

Lord, I don't know what tomorrow will bring,
I just know you will guide my way.
Lord, I don't know why I have battles to fight,
I just know you will protect me today.

Lord, I don't know how to stop my heartache,
I just know you hold me in your arms.
Lord, I don't know why I have so many tears,
I just know you keep me from all harms.

Lord, I don't know what still may lie ahead.
I just know you will hold on to my heart.
Lord, I don't know why my body is so weak,
I just know from me you will never part.

Lord, I don't know why I am always afraid,
I just know you won't leave me alone.
Lord, I don't know what I'm going to do,
I just know I won't have to do it on my own.

NEVER LET ME FORGET

Lord thank you for the heavenly beauty you send my way.
It begins with the glowing opening and closing of each day.
I'm constantly amazed at the lovely greatness you send.
The sky takes my breath away just like the hug of a friend.

The joy of flowers, birds and nature are all around to behold.
Lord, simply stopping to smell your roses renews my soul.
The churning gulf meets the sand with the waves in between.
It is truly an inspiring yet spectacular and a relaxing scene.

I hear the rustle of the wind that forcefully bends some trees.
The swaying of flowers is gently moved by the soft breeze.
The white puffy clouds are always changing and floating by.
It complements the view of the gulf with the magnificent sky.

Each day break starts intensely bright and pristine and new.
Everything is so refreshed and renewed by the morning dew.
Never let me take for granted all the beauty you have created.
Or all the times you tenderly held my hand and on me waited.

Do not allow me to forget or be too busy to take time to see.
Or not notice or be unaware of all the things you give to me.
Great is the luxury of family and friends lovely in many ways.
Thank you dear Lord for the splendor you send to all my days.

If Only I First Talk To God

Life is sometimes too busy to do all I could.
Things don't always happen like they should.
Sometimes I'm too occupied to listen or to hear.
Then God sends a person in need to linger near.

I have much to do or too tired to even recognize.
The pain or hurt or grief is in someone else's eyes.
Too busy to see a need or take some time to care.
Forgetting that time means a lot with one to share.

I often do not pay attention to a tear behind a smile.
I just concentrate on many other things all the while.
Too much is wrong with this picture and life's race.
I must ask God for forgiveness in some quiet place.

Then I will have time to pause at the end of each day.
I can try to lighten someone's troubles in a small way.
I will be able to hear God's plan and the use for me.
So I can hear a broken heart and their tears can see.

Oh never let my life again so busy or complicated be.
That other one's pain and problems I can't read or see.
I can be and say what I was sent here all along to do.
If only I first talk to God before starting anything new.

LORD, I NEED YOUR HELP

All of my strength has gone so far away.
Lord, I need your help especially today.
My faith is strong but my body is so weak.
Lord, just to my heart could you speak?

I struggle with my heavy sorrow every day.
Can I have some hope along the way?
So confused and don't know where to turn,
Lord, I'm giving to you all of my concerns.

I am so weak I can't keep going on alone.
Lord, can you show me the way to keep on?
I am so sad and miserable over my bitter loss.
Lord, only you can help me carry my cross.

I know I should not doubt or ever be afraid.
Lord, then your answers came as I prayed.
I thank you dear Lord, for ever being so near.
You calm all my fears and wipe away my tears.

HELLO GOD

I have so many times of fear and doubt.
Lord, hold to my hand and turn me about.
Thank you for the present of friends so dear.
You sent to me to be all around and so near.

Help me Lord to try and maybe understand.
All trouble, pain and hurt of this great land.
Lord, please help me always to proudly stand.
Make me be mindful of others as only you can.

Thank you for my family you gave and their love.
I know I can't shed a tear that's not known above.
The greater the burden, the more we need you God.
You always know all and see too with a loving nod.

You have no limit to the removing of my heavy load.
While here on earth we all stumble along life's road.
Remind me to give all of it to you to share and bear.
Lord, please keep me forever within your loving care.

KNEEL AND PRAY

Sometimes it would seem clear to me.
That God feels so very far away.
And my life is as tough as it can be,
Cause I forgot to kneel and pray.

The days are filled with trouble and pain.
Feelings of despair are with me all day.
Problems and strife seem to fall like rain,
Cause I forgot to kneel and pray.

Just as it seems I can't take anymore.
God gently reminds He is not far away,
And will send more blessings than before,
When I remember to kneel and pray.

With Him, I will not ever walk alone.
If only on Him all of my burdens I will lay.
More peace and joy than I've ever known
Are mine to have when I kneel and pray.

Through each and every stress my life brings,
God's presence and promise is not far away.
I give all my needs to the King of Kings.
It makes my life whole, when I kneel and pray

Peace Comes From Knowing

The dreary shadows begin to fall all over the land.
No matter what, we are led by the Master's hand.
We have only a little longer in this old world to stay.
Then all the troubles and pain will finally pass away.

There is only a little time for suffering and grief left.
Everyone's sickness and difficulties will end at death.
If one could live their entire life totally problem free.
They would not have reason to go to bended knee.

Yet one would have missed the love of God in prayer.
A life lived without the kind trust of God for every care.
Not ever knowing the feeling of strength to all endure.
Or having answers to prayer when all things were unsure.

At times life sends some of the greatest disappointments.
Everything is for a reason, for His plan and appointments.
All troubles grow smaller and slowly begin to disappear.
If one recognizes that with God one has nothing to fear.

There isn't any limit to the number of times one can pray.
Everyone is blessed with the freedom of prayer all day.
God is near and truly provides for our every single need.
Whether a joy, trial, trouble, blessing or some kind deed.

No situation anyone will ever have will be to face all alone
Peace is from knowing God in Heaven is on His throne.
Faith and trust in God is ample to drive away every fear.
This reassuring thought allows hope to ever remain near.

Elaine Long

GOD IS ALWAYS AROUND IN MANY FORMS

When you are fiercely trying not to sit down and cry.
So many things happen and you are barely getting by.
Life is hard to face and has way too much to bear.
Just remember the best solution is found in a prayer.

When the days are bad and your back is at the wall.
Problems and worries keep coming and on you fall.
God may seem distant and especially when you pray.
Then he sends dear friends to bring you a better day.

I believe in angels, the kind that only God can send.
God gives them to us, simply to be valued friends.
One's life can be blessed with only an angel or two.
An understanding loyalty they always have for you.

Everything in your life seems to keep falling apart.
You feel all alone and carrying a shattered heart.
It helps to remember God's promises from above.
No matter what or when, God is with us with love.

Dawn will break tomorrow no matter what you say.
The sun you may not see but it still rises every day.
When you least expect it the sun will shine its rays.
It is sent from the God of love to brighten our way.

IT MAY NOT BE YOUR WAY

When life gives you something you do not understand.
Trouble and problems meet you almost on every hand.
God is the mighty King and is the master of everything.
Lean on him for strength at times sent on angels wings.

He will lift you up high on the strong wings of his love.
Place all of your problems on him who came from above.
Your greatest victories are still ahead and not in the past.
Each day holds new ideas and opportunities if you ask.

It may not be your anticipated way, but it is God's way.
He had a solution for it before a problem arose any day.
You would not still be remaining down here on this earth.
Except God has some special reason yet for your worth.

Without a burden; one may never have become aware.
The wonderful feeling enjoyed by God's love and care.
One never knows what might be or almost have been.
For only God knows the how and the why and the when.

Until one has stumbled or has fell into the way of harm.
They never have felt comfort and safety in God's arms.
God promised a safe landing; not a routine or easy trip.
He will forever be the all-knowing Captain of life's ship.

A secure faith in God will drive away even your worst fear.
Always fully trust the Lord to wipe away every single tear.
His blessings constantly shower over us like a gentle rain.
He is always near even when the sunshine appears again.

Elaine Long

THINGS NOT SEEN

Things felt by the heart cannot be touched or even seen.
Try to see or hold love and you will know just what I mean.
One can't see a memory unless it is inside of the mind's eye.
Nor can one always see the things that might make one cry.

When somebody loves one and takes them into the heart.
It starts to grow into a beautiful thing right from the start.
All the feelings and throbs of being in love engulf the mind.
These are examples of things felt but the hand can't find.

Can one hold on to a friendship in the palm of one's hand?
It is not possible and it is doubtful anyone ever will or can.
Courage can't be captured and locked deep inside of a bag.
One's faith can't be gathered up and labeled with a red tag.

Love given or received becomes a memory held very dear.
Though love can't be seen, there is nothing about it to fear.
Even if the one that gave love has left for a brand new home.
Treasures of sweet memories keep one from being so alone.

Things one can't try to explain or seem to talk about so much.
Those are the things that are important and our hearts touch.
One's conscience can't be plucked out and all thrown away.
It lives down in one's soul and now and then it saves the day.

One does not see the air but that is vital for life every second.
No one ever sees pain but daily with it some have to reckon.
Grief; the monster is felt so deeply although it remains unseen.
In the heart it does very much damage by being ugly and mean.

Joy is never viewed but goodness, it brings such great cheer.
So does the thought of someone who will forever remain dear.
One can't see God but yet we know He is always really there.
Someday we will see Him and He will then remove every care.

Heaven and all of its glory are things we aren't yet able to see.
Our loved ones are there and mean so very much to you and me.
The best things in life have a reason to remain unseen and free.
It's a part of God's perfect plan and that answer is enough for me.

Steady Faith Saw Me Through

I cried out aloud one day, "Dear Lord, I just don't understand."
So much help I needed to try to see or understand His plan.
I was heart sick, and my daily existence often in great despair.
Such an aching need for help I had and for someone to share.

Worry and fear consumed my days and was even worse at night.
An overwhelming dread was around and sleep was not in sight.
I was drained, weary and fatigued and all of my hope was gone.
There were times I wondered how much longer I could go on.

A heavy heart and weak strength were some obstacles in my way.
In desperation, I gave up and turned it over to the Lord one day.
He was just waiting for me to call and quickly took over the task.
My aching heart, with dread and worries, He gathered up so fast.

He handed them to His angel with all the instructions so complete.
His chosen accepted all the pieces and doubts; with a smile so sweet.
The Lord blessed and showed His one everything to say and to do.
Then never leaving my heart alone, a steady faith saw me through.

A hug or grief felt words with a smile and if needed, a tender touch.
The things said remain a part of my heart and certainly mean so much.
I do not know why I was given love from Heaven and to know the feel.
For through one dear angel, God showed me His love is great and real.

To give all the details correctly or to express the feeling is impossible to say.
I cannot forget the God sent one changing my view that day in many ways.
But I plan to thank God in person when my final day here on earth is done.
I know I was so richly blessed by God to have been loaned this special one.

FAITH TESTED?

A writer and teacher are in this suspected wisdom and fame.
He is such a knowledgeable expert; I can't disclose his name.
He once wrote that his faith is tested many times every day.
Each day has problems or obstacles that would get in his way.

He said actually it is more times than he would like to confess.
At the least little thing, his faith in God is so clouded by stress.
He became miserable and betrayed and in great distress too.
It causes him turmoil and makes him wonder just what to do.

Really I am surprised such an admission like this came to light
I do not feel like my faith in God is tested in the day or at night.
My path may grow weary and my view of surviving it grows dim.
My strength may fail, but I never lose my faith or my trust in Him.

God is always in the same place and is near and lives in my heart.
If one loses their faith in God, it isn't His fault but only on their part.
Some earthly promise may not be kept, but that it is not faith related.
When a secret is told, my patience, but not my faith may be irritated.

If pain or grief comes my way, my faith does not go on a furlough.
I may wonder why God has allowed this weight to torment me so.
But my faith is as stable today as when it all began a long time ago.
My unwavering faith in God is what keeps me going and this I know.

He is the anchor of my faith and He holds on to my body and soul.
Even if my passage is tough, my faith in Him is always in control.
Such a painful vacuum of emptiness is left when a loved one dies.
Yet it is tempered by my faith in God and heaven beyond the skies.

I will keep my lowly life, for here I have enough faith for every need.
Knowing no matter whatever may come, my faith will always succeed.
It seems to me the only way to have faith enough and some to share.
It is to be in touch with God all day long in something called prayer.

Elaine Long

DON'T GIVE ME PRAISE

Before you would smile or nod and think that I act sweet.
Or decide that I did anything someone would find so neat.
You may feel these are some kind or thoughtful things I do.
Just let me try and explain the real truth to each one of you.

I am not any different from everyone else you may know.
Or anybody you see on every journey or place you may go.
God's loving kindness transports me in each and every day.
His gift to me may make you think I am unique in some way.

Don't give me the praise for anything good I may do or say.
God gives me the ideas or thoughts to help one along the way.
It lets me show compassion, hope or lighten one's heavy load.
Or to walk for a time with someone down their sorrowful road.

Simply a kind word said, or a heartfelt card, shoulder, or a call.
Perhaps even a rhyming word or two will help as shadows fall.
I never know what thought may come into my heart and mind.
I only feel it is God through me being compassionate and kind.

He blessed me with any sympathetic, caring trait I have to give.
If I can be of any service and help you move easily in life to live.
Don't give me praise for word or deed I may be led to say or do.
A great Master in Heaven lays it on my heart to pass onto you.

I hope I made a difference, Dear Lord even in some small way.
Please allow them to see it is because you are in my heart to stay.
May the contribution through me be only to glorify you on earth.
Let it never in any way be to credit me or be taken as my worth.

Please allow me only to do the things which give you the praise.
So my life will only honor you in some way the rest of my days.
Thank you Lord, you allowed me to share with others your love.
A love so wonderful could have only come from Heaven above.

I KNOW WHERE I HAVE BEEN

As I walk on alone throughout this life real slow.
I depend on the Lord to bless me wherever I go.
All my needs will be met for the Bible tells me so.
I do not ask how or even have any need to know.

He walked with me long before I ever got this far.
His blessings and love have led me across each bar.
If I am lonely and weak and feeling so very sad.
I name my blessings and see again how many I had.

I know where I have been and what got me through.
My pain and grief have not even been told to a few.
Turning upside down and changing my world too.
My experience was mine and my troubles were too.

Everyone has their own story to remember and tell.
Some are good and others have just walked in hell.
It is not the story or path that matters so very much.
It is really how one handles the opportunity of such.

I can ponder and remember and certainly just guess.
Everything in each one's life is really just one big test.
No one has ever broken a shoulder carrying their load.
For all the weight was on the inside waiting to explode.

Many a fearful mile over ruts and stones are so rough.
There were times when the events of my life were tough.
To complain about or feel sorry, there just wasn't any time.
Looking around I saw others with heavier loads than mine.

My strength and stamina were precious gifts from above.
What carried me through all my dark days was God's love.
All I've given for anyone, or will ever do as my time goes on.
It comes from God's love and power that is always so strong.

GOD AND GOD'S BLESSINGS

GOD UNDERSTANDS AND LISTENS

When sorrow or trouble comes and it almost always will.
Then all of the roads of life seem so rough and turn uphill.
As the anxiety rages and panic storms over you and it will.
Breaths labored and the heart has an unusual painful chill.

When pain or sickness overtakes you and pressure builds.
As it feels like you are alone and no one is aware and it will.
The lonesome valley one walks through in a time of distress.
May be a test of strength and faith would be my best guess.

Trouble and difficulty remind us that only on God to depend.
It is He who can soothe the soul and make all heartaches end.
Ask all the questions though the answers will not come for all.
God is compassionate and will give comfort if on Him you call.

God knows all and to each of us He reaches out a tender hand.
Let him take away all the pain and suffering for He understands.
He endured His broken heart long before our misery ever came.
Ask Him to heal the heart, though never expect it to be the same.

The tremendous storm of sorrow ends and leaves some relief.
Only then does one realize they reached the other side of grief.
Grief is battled, wrestled and endured before it's finally survived.
More than a few times one just wonders if it will leave them alive.

Remember all of the grief will never completely end or go away.
With God's help we learn to live with and in spite of it each day.
Give Him all the pain and suffering asking in Jesus' holy name.
Have faith my friend and peace in your heart God will proclaim.

All the Other Blessings

From before we are born, our destiny has been plotted.
The right amount of love and sadness has been allotted.
God knows and has plans for each soul that he makes.
A clear blueprint is there for whatever journey life takes.

God doesn't cause things to happen to anyone of his flock.
I suspect He allows situations so we on his door will knock.
Each one's journey through life always has a reason for it.
I believe He never meant for us to be alone or in fear to sit.

Because He sees and knows all, He fills our every need.
Often times He uses us to help others in some good deed.
He directs our lives in special orchestrated chains of events.
If an angel appears to help, they are always Heaven sent.

He knows all of our needs long before any problem we face.
The very best part is He is by our side no matter the case.
If we had no pain in our life would we ever know His grace?
I guess we would not remember; our trust on Him to place.

All of our friends and their blessings we would never see.
If in all of our lives some rain or clouds there would not be.
I would probably change many things if I had the chance.
Then for all the rest of my life I would celebrate and dance.

But I would miss the other blessings God has planned for me.
Friends and support and kindness of others I would not see.
The perfect one is in control and thankfully will be forevermore.
I believe more blessings than we have known are still in store.

Elaine Long

I Think God Gave Us Love

Our heart is involved in every type emotion we face.
It begins in the heart and love moves at a fast pace.
Love can withstand and endure the most awful blow.
That love also supports and sustains if one feels low.

Sometimes painful stuff is more than a heart can take.
Pain from grief enters the heart and can make it break.
Love can shatter a heart, yet it can also cause it to sing.
Love is eternal, and love will survive all kinds of things.

Compassion or sympathy comes from the heart in love.
All the emotions were put into the heart by God above.
Concern and understanding were packed in there too.
Kindness is sincere love in all that one can say or do.

As a heart has testing or some surgery performed on it.
It is understandable why all the emotions also take a hit.
Faith and trust in God gives all permission to move on.
Life may be changed, if it is His will, and worry all gone.

I think God gave us love for the enjoyment of everyone.
God's love and grace is the best blessing under the sun.
Thank you Lord, You make our hearts so strong and wise.
It is attached to a lot more than we humans can ever realize.

Count My Blessings

I never can even begin all my blessings to count.
Every day, my blessings will upon another mount.
No matter what the day may bring God blesses me.
Some days are for a time the blessing I can't see.

Some of life's burdens are just so heavy to bear.
It's easy to wonder why and if anyone does care.
Troubles and heartaches follow each other non-stop.
Stress or worry or pain or sorrow continuing to drop.

Everything happens for a reason that's fact and true.
And God is right there beside me to see it through.
Whatever the circumstances sometimes I later see.
In all that strife there was a blessing there for me.

It may have come in the strength of one dear friend.
Who held on until the heart finally began to mend.
It could have arrived in the way of another safe day.
A loved one died but knowing their pain went away.

No better friend than God could one ever hope to find.
He is gracious and loving and compassionate and kind.
I cannot count high enough to total all my blessings.
Everyday more come and with them so many lessons.

All blessings come from the paradise of Heaven above.
A blessing is another reminder of God's constant love.
Without his blessings in my life all my efforts would fail.
Any attempt to anything right would only be one tall tale.

The love of family and special friends are blessings too.
For without them and their sweet care what would I do?
These special blessings in my heart I will forever keep.
I thank God each night for my blessings before I sleep.

Elaine Long

ONLY GOD KNOWS

The initial plans for an affair had been made a long time back.
Family members were really excited as they began to pack.
The varied dishes of food were coming together in full swing.
All seemed to be going just fine until that phone began to ring.

An undiagnosed illness was giving concern and a great big scare.
It gave a fear of contact to something quite simple or perhaps rare.
Those with low resistance had simply too much to risk and to lose.
Sadly and regretfully canceling the meal was all they could choose.

The plans made became the plans withdrawn and all within the hour.
The disappointment and tears quickly turned everyone's mood to sour.
A hasty change of direction became the only solution there could be.
On beyond Thanksgiving the test results would still remain a mystery.

A great many feelings of isolation and sadness were felt on the inside.
Outside, a meeting left arms aching for the hugs that had to be denied.
Yet came bonding and renewing of closeness to a brother and his son.
It had left a good feeling of much thanksgiving when the day was done.

Finally, good news came a day late and the worry was no longer there.
The illness so feared had not developed but all had nerves to repair.
To understand why or a reason for it, one may never see or know.
An explanation, or the message embedded inside may not ever show.

It is hard to endure some frustrating events and within it to find a lesson.
Or to face adversity and still remember in everything there is a blessing.
Maybe some once reserved family members will begin again to bond.
A few toughened hearts may soften as if touched with a magic wand.

The best giving of thanks may be how much family to each one means.
It reminds everyone only God knows best and is always on the scene.
May the much loved family members grow to be even more special too.
The simple reality of not knowing what tomorrow will bring holds so true.

God's plan is never bad, or late, or uncertain, nor can it ever be wrong.
Sometimes it takes a little while to renew a faith which was all but gone.
Only God knows why and how the reasons will come together at last.
Nothing or anyone to his wonderful love and grace can ever surpass.

THE SPECIAL BLESSING

There comes a time in one's life that they realize.
Those you value the most in life by their heart ties.
Some never last and there is a reason they never will.
Others won't for their excuses certainly make me ill.

A few will always remain entwined inside the heart.
These will just stay in your life and be a precious part.
Do not worry about the ones you leave in your past.
God always has a reason why they do not seem to last.

It could be a guardian angel sent to assist in your life.
Possibly it's a special friend coming to divert your strife.
Maybe it is a person touched by God and then sent.
One never knows just why a sympathetic heart is lent.

But the special blessing of having a true friend is great.
A splendid connection and never casually be in or take.
No amount of time can shake the bond that lies there.
True friends have angel wings and address every care.

It feels exactly just like the Calvary had ridden in fast.
The worries and problems and pain recede into the past.
God's generous love is seen and felt if a friend is there.
A friend takes the cares and gives them to God in prayer.

GOD WALKS WITH ME

You know God never gives us too much to bear.
Sometimes we forget how much He does care.
Remember the worst time in your life and recall.
How you had enough strength to get through it all.

How such worry and sacrifice went on day after day.
Yet each day you had stamina and found your way.
On and on and yet you did not ever stop or wear out.
Not knowing how you managed without much doubt.

Remember how calmly you went about all your tasks?
Yet there were some questions you just knew not to ask.
Not ever thinking of yourself or the stress toll upon you.
But ever willing to do whatever was needed for others too.

That somehow to the loved one you filled their every need.
All that time you were the recipient of God's love indeed.
His love and care is sufficient enough for me and for you.
He is aware and near and in everything we attempt to do.

It takes a while after an event to be able to see or to hope.
How we face the tomorrows and learn exactly how to cope.
My mind is weak and I don't always know what is best.
Yet I know my God is there with me in every single test.

God walks with me no matter the weather or the terrain.
He is there in trouble, illness, worry or death or great pain.
Maybe now most of the trials have all finally passed away.
Hopefully now I have become a better person in every way.

Elaine Long

FOR US HE WILL FOREVER CARE

I sincerely believe that everything has some reason.
As in the Bible, each part of our life has a season.
Nothing happens except it is in and of God's plan.
He simply holds all our needs in His gracious hand.

Whether it is sickness, worry or death He knows.
On this earth, we know not why or how He chose.
Through every hurdle in our life, He is fully aware.
We are his creation and will forever be in his care.

He is always beside us, for help all we have to do is ask.
He will take the burden and give strength for the task.
All the times we are our weakest, God is the strongest.
When others have left our side, He remains the longest.

I have not the answers why things happen, as they will.
How events in life can cause the spine to have a chill.
I know God sends friends to walk along our uneasy way.
They were probably close by all the while; until one day.

God tapped their shoulder and pointed them to a need.
There is a reason for that and it too is heartfelt indeed.
Friends are true blessings more than we can often realize.
We should look at them more closely through God's eyes.

God is there all the time gently, quietly looking after me.
I know not why things happen, yet in God my faith shall be.
One day in Heaven, I feel He will explain it all to you and me.
I know for now, God has a reason and that is enough for me.

I Am Blessed

I have a safe roof that is all intact covering my head.
Not a lot of problems have I but many comforts instead.
I am blessed with having good health and ample agility.
My wants, now and then seem to outweigh my ability.

My good family genes and morals are so many to uphold.
I have such fond memories to carry with me as I grow old.
Usually for most of my time now I simply call it all my own.
I can stay up late or rise up real early just to see the dawn.

All of these treasures and riches I can call my own but yet.
There are many other blessings that surpass these like a jet.
My friends and loved ones are very sweet blessings to me.
No matter where I am or what I'm in they are there for me.

I am blessed to have my friends and loved ones all so near.
Each time I greet them it warms my heart for each is a dear.
Knowing angel wings hover around that others cannot see.
I am thankful to God for the blessings He showers over me.

Why God gave me many blessings; in this life I will not know.
Unable to count them now but I plan to in heaven should I go.
I am aware of the special family and friends He has given me.
My cup and saucer run over and I thank Him from my knees.

GOD'S POWER

All of the months of worry had filled our lives with dread.
A terrible diagnosis revealed that soon he would be dead.
Only after the second opinion allowed any hope to return.
We sure had very much more to endure and yet to learn.

A repair or fix operation was soon scheduled to be done.
Another chance for life came on his birthday; what a pun.
The long operation was without a problem until the end.
His heart had failed to resume beating on its own again.

As a nurse said the doctor was waiting, oh I was so afraid.
Those awful words he stated, on my mind has yet to fade.
He said, "I have no idea of the why, nor can I offer hope."
I knew I could not carry this burden alone or try to cope.

Up until then I had only thought that my faith was strong.
However I would shortly discover I was entirely wrong.
The call for a prayer chain went out for strength and grace.
We asked for strength for him and for what we had to face.

I'll never know how many prayers were offered in that hour.
I do know on that day in the hospital, we felt God's power.
Then I saw the strength of my faith was not ever in doubt.
Every day since then I have known God's mercy is all about.

Though we faced a sure death and all the hope was withheld.
There was calm and peace felt as we waited until all was well.
Death would not be cheated and arrived at a much later date.
But we endured because God had strengthened us in our wait.

Solutions we pray for may not often arrive, but faith will grow.
God is always in charge, I felt his love there on that day I know.
His reasons are with a purpose and are always correct and pure.
My strength in this body may waver but my faith in God is sure.

Fabulous Gifts and Special Blessings

Looking back with emotion as the year comes to an end.
I was waiting and anticipating for the New Year to begin.
The number of blessings I have received in this past year.
They are so uncountable like all the raindrops falling here.

Each year begins and ends on the faces of all I hold dear.
I have been showered with sweet love for the entire year.
They were funny or serious, good or bad days but overall.
It was a sweeter year of heart feeling of many I can recall.

Dear Lord I thank you for the precious gift of your love.
This emotion must have been created in Heaven above.
Love makes everything and everyday worth living it is true.
But most of all Lord, it is one of many blessings from you.

My loved ones are fabulous gifts and special blessings too.
I am so thankful for their presence the whole year through.
Without them to hold on to would bring an awful disaster.
To have them near is a taste of the rapture in the hereafter.

Thankfully only God knows what awaits us in the year ahead.
Only our faith in Him will prevail when all else has been said.
He is not the God of a party but He is the only and all being.
He had a final say on His creation and now on all He is seeing.

All of the problems in this world today can really get one down.
In everything else God always knows what's best I have found.
So I think the solution to all of our problems is to ask in prayer.
Then we will never let anything interfere with God's loving care.

Elaine Long

TROUBLE CLUTTERS THE MIND

When some days are just the pits and nothing goes right.
All problems mount up and chores run on into the night.
The big list of promises made and broken spoils the day.
Hurt feelings and disappointments just get into the way.

When fear or anxiety comes, it makes the walls close in.
After a long sleepless night the same mood starts again.
The day will collect more problems while it moves along.
It seems if all trust and hope have disappeared and gone.

Sometimes trouble clutters the mind with so much difficulty.
It is hard to be thankful for or any hope in the future to see.
When nothing else is going alright and the mood is so low.
Take a pen and tablet and start writing down all you know.

Write down your blessings one by one before a day is done.
You will find yourself awake really late counting each one.
It is about finding blessings amid a heart full of pain and woe.
No matter how bad one feels, blessings around us ever flow.

Count them one by one or even in twos or in dozens galore.
The number continues to grow and at the end, so many more.
So many blessings go unnoticed than are counted to be sure.
Like a background of blue sky with puffy white clouds so pure.

Silent beauty is a sunrise streaming on a sea of dancing waves.
Brilliant collections of God made accumulations deep in caves.
Things overlooked or unseen are special blessings in every way.
Looking inward often finds so much to be thankful for each day.

The ability and capacity for love is above all the other blessings.
All of the aspects of love provide us with many countless lessons.
Problems are removed by God's mercy and that never grows old.
God is love and He is the provider of all of the blessings we hold.

GOD SEES THE END

For every situation there is always some hope.
In time of trouble it is God who helps one cope.
Don't give into total despair or fall under the load.
God may turn it into a blessing on down the road.

He is the strength for the weaknesses of all kind.
Yes He is also the best friend one could ever find.
God sees the end long before anything ever begins.
His love is forever sure and quite generous to lend.

The road may be winding, rough and very long.
God walks with us every step for we are not alone.
There are times when the worries seem to over flow.
God gives us many chances for character to grow.

He gives many blessings and is there in time of need.
He is present beside us always offering a kind deed.
If we call to God He will give us strength for our course.
Throughout the storm or night He is the calming force.

If the worst thing that could ever happen comes to call.
At those times when we feel like we have given our all.
When we want to give up and throw in the towel and quit.
We can look around and see God beside us where we sit.

The glories of Heaven one day He will show to me and you.
Removing the pain we had felt before He touched us too.
We are never beyond the reach of our dear God's grace.
The day will come when we can thank Him face to face.

Elaine Long

STRENGTH FROM OTHERS

I have seen and felt much misery at different times in life.
Some came before and during and then after I was a wife.
I don't pretend to think I had more than anyone else found.
Nor do I think I handled it any better than anyone around.

But I will say this much and I do mean it with all my heart.
If not for God, family and friends being near from the start.
Without all the strength they have provided along the way.
My life and mind would truly not be as stable as it is today.

Unwavering love and help from others has seen me this far.
It will also keep me secure until I meet God beyond the star.
God is the one who deserves all the thanks and my devotion.
He gave to me family and friends with the love to fill an ocean.

Sometimes people are so consumed with the grief and woe.
That it becomes so hard to remember God still loves them so.
I have no answers as to why my trust in Him has never waned.
His love always was and is given to me over and over again.

Thank you God, for making me feel so special in many ways.
I don't know why I was chosen to feel much love every day.
Still I know there is a good reason dear Lord for all you do.
Only when we meet in Heaven will you tell me the why too.

BEACON OF TRANQUILITY

Sitting alone and unnoticed was an angel night light.
Its sole purpose was in the dark to shine real bright.
It was plugged in an outlet at the end of a hall way.
The outlet was loose, so the angel in darkness lay.

There for months the little cherub sat quietly in recluse.
Seemingly not needed or having any purpose or use.
Then one night while its owner lay in distress close by.
Her gasping prevented her from enough oxygen to cry.

All of a sudden that little angel night light began to show.
It lit up all the bedroom and hall with an uncanny glow.
As if in some reassurance that everything would be alright.
It gave hope as she lay there gasping all through the night.

Little by little the panic lessened and morning came again.
Something had changed with less coughing and such pain.
God and His angels were there on the morning of that day.
She called the doctor's office and was told to head that way.

As she turned around to get dressed and to the doctor go,
The little angel night light had suddenly lost its great glow.
Since that night the little angel has again in darkness stood.
Somehow she knew then without a mission, it always would.

Yet it is comforting to know an angel is on guard and close by.
It will always be her beacon of tranquility sent from on high.
That night will long remain in her mind with a comforting thought.
There will not be a reason to fear anything or again be distraught.

It had no rhyme or reason why it turned on by itself and then off.
Only God could have caused that little angel glow for her so soft.
He is nearby and watching over us with angels wherever we go.
That night her future was changed from death to life in the glow.

Elaine Long

MY GUARDIAN ANGEL LIGHT AGAIN

Last night was the first time since my fall that I was alone.
I have been much pampered since I had broken a bone.
Dear friends bathed me in love and much help and care.
For the want or need of anything, well I just didn't dare.

On the third night after a balancing act which didn't go well.
This was the first night to spend at home alone since I fell.
My guardian angel night light was there to light up for me.
It has no rhyme nor reason as to when it turns on you see.

It glowed brightly that night to protect me until the next day.
All through the night it illuminated the room and lit my way.
I got up the last time not very long before the daylight call.
The gleam of the angel still cast a warm ray down the hall.

But just before the break of dawn, the angel's glow went out.
As to who turned it on and then off I will never have a doubt.
The night time had ended and again all was safe and well.
My little angel light was on guard all night as far as I can tell.

God's love goes far beyond the night light shining at my door.
He is always my protector and helper and will be forever more.
The daylight approached and sunshine safely came again.
I know He had watched over me all night for He is my friend.

TIME WELL SPENT

I do not know what the cause or whatever the reason.
It does not even change from one season to season.
Most of my nights I know it are not worth going to bed.
It is incurable insomnia, or that is what the doctor said.

The sleep escapes me as the hours slowly creep on by.
All my time does not fly at night, and for that I can testify.
The clock can rest without any fear for the whole night.
My eyes will keep a watch over it with all my might.

The naps are followed by long periods of time to think.
Morning finally comes but I am way short of forty winks.
I'm ready to start my day before the sun or day is awake.
At least I know that for any appointment I will not be late.

A good thing I find from this is not having any bad dreams.
One has to sleep in order to have dreams or so it seems.
I don't worry or even fret over time that I just can't sleep.
And I sure don't waste any time counting all those sheep.

My body gets rest in between tossing and turning in bed.
Thoughts of the day are on my mind of things yet ahead.
Counting blessings and talking to God is time well spent.
All that time for prayer and thanksgiving is heaven sent.

HEAVEN:
OUR ETERNAL HOME

WHERE IS HEAVEN

From childhood, I have heard of Heaven's story.
God is in Heaven with angels, mansions and glory.
I do believe it is true for the Holy Bible tells us so.
When we die as believers, Heaven is where we go.

I always assumed Heaven was past the clouds above.
Jesus ascended there to his Father waiting in love.
He slowly disappeared from his sad disciple's view.
So that much we read and believe to be fact and true.

I recently heard someone explain the event this way.
He talked of out of body experiences happening today.
Reciting, "Eyes had not seen and ears not yet heard."
This point he made was based on God's Holy Word.

If spiritual eyes were opened rather than our mortal eyes,
What sights would be around us that we could recognize?
Are the loved ones who died all around us here below?
Do they stay with us all the time and everywhere we go?

Is that why at times we can feel then so close and near?
Then at other times we feel as if we have nothing to fear.
Could that explain when the death angel comes to call?
A dying one sees deceased family members on the wall?

Have their eyes been opened and sights to them revealed?
They can see God and all the majesty no longer concealed.
Wherever it is; Heaven will now be their home forevermore.
They will watch and wait for us to come in Heaven's door.

I have no answers, just many questions and without a clue.
So I will not guess what our precious Lord is going to do.
I find it a comforting thought if indeed this might be true.
To think that our loved ones are near in everything we do.

THE ANGELS' CHOIR

It is with and in every breath my Lord allows me to take.
In each and every faltering step I stumble and try to make.
I'm always reminded of the wonderful love of Him on high.
One day I'll thank Him in person when from this world I fly.

In the Lord is my strength and He is always a haven of rest.
He is the one who helps us the most and is the very best.
By God's strong loving grace we can always find our way.
The magnificent entrance of glory will call us home one day.

I have always known this place on earth was not my home.
One day we will be called and not ever again walk on alone.
The shattered dreams and broken hearts will come to an end.
Then for the last time we won't have to get up and try again.

Many times I held on until finally I was at the end of my rope.
It was God who gently picked me up and restored my hope.
When the death angel knocks upon my door and calls for me.
Without even a backward glance I will go in an instant to see.

There will be a great celebration and a welcome home band.
The harps will play with the angels' choir from Heaven's land.
Each of us will go home by God's timing and we won't be late.
All of our loved ones will be waiting to greet us inside the gate.

The master will be dressed in robes of beauty on earth unknown.
He will welcome each one of His children to Him near the throne.
For an eternity to be spent in love and joy and singing His praise.
What a glad reunion which will continue for the rest of our days.

Elaine Long

HOW WONDERFUL IT WILL BE

If you should get to Heaven sometime before I do.
Then I just know that I can really count on you.
Go about shaking hands and hugging loved ones.
Right after you give much thanks to the Holy One.

What a time that will be rejoicing with them one and all.
Greeting those loved ones and friends with a glad call.
You will feast in a land of milk and honey forevermore.
While you watch and wait for me to come in the door.

Though if I am called up into Heaven right before you.
Don't be sad and lonely and wonder what you will do.
When I get to see my Lord face to face I will feel great.
I will be looking for you while I swing on the pearly gate.

Calling out to all loved ones to come and gather round.
Telling them you are on your way and Heaven bound.
Then we will all be together where there is no night fall.
How wonderful it will be to be gathered in by Jesus' call.

Spending eternity surrounded by ones we love the best.
Never to part again or having our faith put to any test.
What a glorious feeling that will be with pain no more.
All suffering and problems will be left at Heaven's door.

Walking and talking with our Lord in a peaceful bliss.
Not once thinking of earth or anything we could miss.
Paradise waits for us where we won't have any cares.
No matter who goes home first, we will meet up there.

More Precious than Diamonds or Pearls

It is different from anything ever experienced on earth.
A priceless value is of an uncountable amount of worth.
It just cannot be compared to anything else of this world.
So much more precious is it than all the diamonds or pearls.

The words have yet to be invented that can describe it well.
Nor can it be characterized as good enough for anyone to tell.
It is quite difficult to explain for it is illusive even to the receiver.
Though unexplainable to most, it is crystal clear to the believer.

Some things are meant to be seen and felt but not ever understood.
Like knowing about Heaven and in the hereafter, and no one should.
Imagine being in the quiet place near to the heart of God on High.
That is the closest thought I can relate it to, this miracle close by.

Most of life is not understood or passed on to either woman or man.
Eyes and ears have not seen or heard, of the things of the holy land.
Yet it would seem at times when events are terrible down here below.
God sees and instructs an angel and then tells them just where to go.

Angel wings are soon heard right near the hurting soul's faltering side.
Being first blest and sent by God, the angel can push all the hurt aside.
It is nearly impossible to explain the feeling the angel will bring along.
It is beyond words except, it is a gift from Heaven, an angel on loan.

Elaine Long

ANY PLACE WILL BE NEAT

A God loving Christian this old girl will forever be.
If you should happen to disagree, then forgive me.
A mansion for me with it finery I may never earn.
Seeing all of my loved ones is not my main concern.

Just a little shack placed somewhere on a back street.
As long as I can meet my Lord, any place will be neat.
I like to see the beginning of a day while it is all new.
Often time I talk to God quite early while there is dew.

I like to do things when I see a need or want to do.
Helping someone else helps me be able to get through.
I don't do showy or the fluffy things like icing on a cake.
The most secretive ideas are the kind I try to do or make.

If the things I find or see to do aren't just quite right.
I ask God for forgiveness when I talk to him at night.
Some things can't be fixed or made to be good as new.
However for everything that matters God answers too.

To reside anywhere in Heaven's glory will be just fine.
Rejoicing with the Lord and loved ones will be divine.
Answers to all questions will be shared with us then.
We will forever live in a place that never has any sin.

The beauty there will not compare to any earthly things.
One of the most pleasant sounds will be angels' wings.
While no shacks in Heaven exist on any golden street.
To reside for eternity in Heaven, any place will be neat.

IT SOUNDS LIKE HEAVEN

I've just been thinking about going home.
Here with the troubles down here below.
It will be great no longer to be here to roam.
There can be no trouble or pain where I go.

When life on this earth ends I will bid adieu.
Then I can finally lay down this heavy load.
Heaven will magnificently come into my view
It will be no trouble to walk the golden road.

There with all friends and family I will ever be.
Forever singing praises to God and His Son.
Hearing the answers revealed at Jesus' knee.
The close of an eternal day will never be done.

It will just be a fantastic paradise for us to see.
Angels and harps will be such beauty to behold.
The splendor and glory will last for all of eternity.
We will sit there and marvel and never grow old.

My mind here on earth cannot imagine the sight.
Can you envision seeing Heaven's pearly gates?
I long to see love ones and hug with my might.
Oh, it just sounds like Heaven and I can't wait.

The music and singing beyond any wistful dream.
Such grand scenery will take an eternity to explore.
I'll live forever with God and all of the redeemed.
And I know that it will last and last forevermore.

Elaine Long

FAMILY,
VALUES AND TEACHINGS

HAND IN HAND WITH GOD

It has been twenty years ago today since she went away.
The void left by her passing is quite strongly felt today.
She touched so many lives in example and by teaching.
Her success in training will continue to be far reaching.

She walked hand and hand with God each day she lived.
No matter what she gave she always had more to give.
Her tireless dedication to all others was a heavenly trait.
A heart of gold, thoughtful beyond belief, she was first rate.

Her cooking brought warmth to the inside and deep within.
How I would like to be able to eat at her table once again.
Patience was a virtue and her generosity was full measure.
Memories of her are so priceless and a precious treasure.

Although I know where she is and now she wears a crown.
Many days I stood alone aching for her sweet voice sound.
In my heart she will remain and forever fill a special place.
That grand lady was a model of love and faith and grace.

I never heard any person say anything negative about her.
She was a blessing to all; we didn't know how lucky we were.
Now she rejoices in Heaven's glory where she longed to go.
She is so happy there but she was Mama and I miss her so.

MAMA'S HANDS

As Mother's day nears; it opens the pages of my memory bank.
For many things I will always have my mother's hands to thank.
Mama's hands held some kind of magic in all the work they did.
For there wasn't anything she couldn't do when I was a little kid.

Those well-worn hands loved and taught and cooked and fed.
I was not sent, but into the church and by those hands was led.
Hands often folded in prayer asking God to keep watch over us.
She pressed out the wrinkles in clothes and life without any fuss.

She gently wiped away tears after every hurt or any kind of pain.
The school lunch bags she packed were anything but just plain.
Those sweet hands could from an empty cupboard make a meal.
Whipping up a cake so fast and long before fancy cooking was real.

Her thoughtful heart was felt in those hands as she gave her all.
They trembled and shook when loneliness or death came to call.
Her hands were worn, creased and raw from work and many chores.
Those same dear hands sewed all the dresses and clothes that I wore.

She painstakingly and lovingly made the dress I wore the day I wed.
I tried to get her to go with me to purchase a readymade one instead.
But she insisted on making it herself and she put love in every stitch.
When it was finished; all the extra work made it look so fancy and rich.

Elaine Long

She had many hard times being a friend, daughter, mother and a wife.
But she always prayed and then conquered every obstacle in her life.
Mama's loving hands left an imprint on each life that they ever touched.
I will always wonder if she really knew that I loved her so very much.

God had his own reasons for creating her into such a fantastic gem.
One day He held out his hand and took her home to Heaven with Him.
Now from memories I have described my sweet mother and her hands.
To have been her child was the best gift found anywhere in this land.

I may have also described your mother somewhere here in these lines.
God makes mothers from special molds and it includes yours and mine.
If my words remind you of your mother and her wonderful hands today.
Take a walk in your book of memories and then happily reminisce away.

DEAR DAD

It's been 20 years ago I said
      Goodbye to you, Dad.
Oh what a terrible day it was,
      It made me so very sad.
You sat down to rest for a while
      and God called your name.
The time since that sad day
      has not been the same.

I heard my Mama say to herself,
      "Oh what will I ever do?"
As I heard her heartbroken word,
      I thought the same thing too!
So many memories still easily flow
      through my busy mind.
Though it has been such a long time
      joys of you are not left behind.

So many things you showed and taught
      to me along the way.
The knowledge that you gave then
      still guides me today.
Truth was your word and was your bond
      as everyone always knew.
Your friends numbered so many,
      enemies not even a few.

Love came first in all you did
      and pride in our family name.
Without those important things,
      life would not be the same.
Thank you Dad for lessons that
      still cast a gentle glow.
They are an influence on my life
      everywhere I go.

          Elaine Long

I Miss Brother

It has been one year since my dear brother had to go away.
So much time has gone by since that awful unexpected day.
The memories have filled my mind of good times of long ago.
Tender moments, temper tantrums, or strength all have a glow.

Each one is a reminder of my loss felt painfully once more.
I miss most of all seeing him standing outside my back door.
We often sat at the table and talked and he liked this time too.
Smiling he accepted and took home a bowl of soup or stew.

I miss the bond we shared by parents and the family name.
Without him now, life just doesn't seem to be quite the same.
He taught me about bugs and frogs and oh yes some snakes.
I loved puppies and baby squirrels and swimming in our lake.

A daily trip after school to check the rabbit boxes in the woods.
Which berries to eat or not, and digging fish bait and other goods.
I learned a lot from one who could have been Daniel Boone's son.
Of dressing turtle, cleaning fish or game he shot with his shotgun.

He always gave me safety tips around the creek and at my house.
I depended on his drop by visits much more after I lost my spouse.
He was nearby and dependable and if needed just down the road.
That was reassuring to me though to him I never shared this load.

If he had a problem or something he did not quite understand.
He would bring it over here and to sister he would timidly hand.
Then he patiently waited for me to explain or fix it if I had a clue.
It seemed he looked to me for help as he had with mama too.

He had a different but excellent idea of important things in his life.
His love of hunting and fishing followed family, his child and wife.
It took precedence over other duties that life ever sent his way.
He worked when needed but fishing was the highlight of any day.

He was quiet and nervous and unsure of himself some times its true.
When upon his bulldozer, he was a pro and knew exactly what to do.
The first year has come and past and without him life has moved on.
His footprint to follow will always remain even though he has gone.

Elaine Long

HER NAME WAS ROSE

Her personality was delightful just like a lovely rose.
With warm smile and soft voice she was named well.
A very good friend sweet and kind as my story goes.
She had many good qualities more than I can ever tell.

Brothers treated her with love and respect and the rest.
She was loved by all who shared a time in life with her.
No matter the job or fishing or hunting she did her best.
Her talents were many and for bad habits, not any no sir.

She married my unruly brother and I asked her one time,
If she thought she needed some more adventure in her life?
Smiling she said, "No I just love him and we will be just fine."
He who would not marry we thought; sure took a fine wife.

So they went; her teaching love and he how to hunt and fish.
Their daughter was blessed with all the qualities of the pair.
She grew up to be as sweet and smart as any parent's wish.
With loving, kind and heart felt qualities that today are so rare.

Then one spring day Rose left without time for a good bye.
God called, she answered, and another angel went upstairs.
He took her in an instant leaving all of us to just wonder why?
Her leaving was sudden, and the pain to nothing did compare.

Husband, sons and daughter left with a deep hole in their heart.
As the unexpected death always has the hardest shock to take.
The utter disbelief and the grief have always been the worst part.
Those first years without her were so painfully difficult to make.

Thirty years and two days later her husband joined her there.
In all that time he had never forgotten what he had and then lost.
A gruff persona tried to hide the fact, for her he did always care.
Now again they are together, when the Jordan River he crossed.

One Very Special Girl

When she was born she looked very much like her Dad.
But that was alright too for he was a good looking lad.
Her quick smile and her laughter were always nearby.
With such a bubbling personality it just made one sigh.
She had a wisp of a body so her actions as quick as a wink.
She could get things done faster than anyone could think.

Her gifted Dad taught to her how to hunt and fish so well.
When she beat him he only pretended to be as mad as hell.
Dad made her tough and called her boy but it did no harm.
Her quiet, graceful Mama just taught her poise and charm.
She was the big apple in her grandparent's hearts and eye.
She gave more joy than she ever received and that is no lie.

Offering love and support after her Mom was taken away.
They loved her more than any deeds or words can ever say.
They thoroughly enjoyed her living with them in those years.
An aunt and uncle did what they could to wipe away her tears.
She soon grew up to be lovely and very sweet and so smart.
The desire to look after animals took her energy and her heart.

Her gift did not need a degree but to a special college she went.
All who knew her talent readily gave their blessings and consent.
She soon graduated with a double degree in compassion and love.
Her natural born ability was something that just came from above.
Then she went to work with one who loved animals just as much.
As a team this pair had a knack for healing eyes with a loving touch.

Time has flown and some joy and sadness have both been known.
Most of the family they once had near now has a brand new home.
The ones left behind have been through many long and difficult tests.
At times the journey was troubled with pain and suffering and no rest.
Having this niece in our midst has made all the difference in the world.
Thank you Dear Lord, for sending to this family one very special girl.

Elaine Long

MUCH TO HIS CREDIT

He is one kind man and one of a kind and real soft hearted guy too.
Everyone can depend on him to go out of his way for me or for you.
Because he had grown up as a poor farm boy, country life was rough.
He learned from the sweat of his brow and he had to grow up tough.

Being a trusted friend and true to his word is to him not ever a game.
He comes from some good genes and wears a treasured family name.
He has jokes and yarns and tales, all of which he likes to spin and tell.
Some of his stories were acquired from many miles covered as well.

I believe it would be correct to label him as one fine traveling man.
He drove big trucks on interstates in every state all across this land.
A big map is etched across his brain of those highways and roads.
He then rode on the iron rail and pulled so many freight train loads.

Rain, sleet, snow or bitter cold, or extreme heat, he always had to go.
He and his wife raised six children well without having much dough.
The children were given more love than some rich kids will ever see.
All of the value of his limitless experiences he gave to them for free.

Much advanced book education he would not have the time to learn.
His traveling and life on the road was a hard way for his living to earn.
So respected and loved is he by all his friends it would be safe to say.
Other than a gift to gab, I never heard anything about him in any way.

He began and rose through the line to be a leader of a respected group.
As the president he did well and he also made his dune buggy do loops.
A dependable leader he set and met goals which before were unreached.
Country bred, and a cross country education gave him wisdom to teach.

This man has much to his credit and life and in so many different ways.
Today is as special to him as he is to us, for it is his seventy-fifth birthday.
Now all this information about him you may wonder how I would know.
The best part of this story is he is my oldest brother, and I love him so.

A Gem of a Lady

She was born up in Tennessee on one January day.
But not for long in the mountains would she play.
Her home soon became on the good Georgia clay.
So it was here for the rest of her life she would stay.
As a teenager she sewed the shirts at a plant or mill.
It was for about fifty years her sewing paid the bills.
She became a part of our family in nineteen sixty two.
For more than forty years I called her my sister too.
Her many and varied talents could fill a big long list.
Cooking, creating, fishing, loving, you can get the gist.
Four fine sons grew up loved and called her mother.
The two step daughters would love her like no other.
Her quick tongue was soft or not if to state her mind.
She also had such a heart of gold and she was so kind.
If she was nearby and on your side; you had a real pal.
Treat family or friend bad and her mood turned foul.
A full of mischief husband she might need to dictate.
Though she always knew what to say or do to motivate.
She loved a good time, those crazy cartoons, or a joke.
To some very good friends, dry humor she might poke.

She nearly always would say exactly what she thought.
Her love, friendship or trust could not ever be bought.
But mostly to another, a dearer friend one couldn't find.
Her support and sweet loyalty was of the sweetest kind.
Opal was her name, and she was a gem without measure.
Being counted as one of her dear friends was a pleasure.
Music was in her soul, and how she could play and sing.
Along with all of her brothers could make the rafters ring.
A long illness took her away from us in two thousand five.
It was a great loss and our grief was severe, I must confide.
I know that nothing since her death has seemed the same.
It is merely not as much fun now playing in life's old game.
One grandson she had taught from birth sitting in her lap.
He seems not to be able without her to adjust or now adapt.
He should realize that he will not ever be just the only one.
All who knew her will constantly miss her and all of her fun.
If she were here today, she would know exactly what to do.
I expect things would change and be entirely different too.
But she is in Heaven now and along with most of her clan.
She is there with them and she is playing in the best band.

WHAT A PRIVILEGE

Life in childhood times was truly so wonderfully sweet.
Not poor in things that mattered and one's life was neat.
Growing up in an age where common sense was a rule.
In the forties and fifties parents didn't raise many fools.

Children made up their own games for entertainment.
Playing checkers, cards, and ball was standard events.
A book mobile or library on wheels was a special treat.
Most common transportation consisted of two big feet.

The sights and sounds of those days fill a memory bank.
Unloading wagons of fresh hay left little time for pranks.
An old farm bell called all the workers in for a big dinner.
Sure made one think they had been declared the winner.

Watermelon cuttings and homemade ice cream was fun.
Simple pleasures for enjoyment and no one carried a gun.
Sunday school attendance was not ever optional but a fact.
Parents made sure children knew how to dress and to act.

Chores were a big part of growing up and all had to share.
Lending a hand was done without hesitation and with care.
Morals and doing right was instilled in little minds real early.
Discipline was administered if the child wanted to act surly.

Respect of self, parents and others was always well taught.
Being kind and helpful to all was a deeply implanted thought.
Great values from childhood made the world a better place.
Those traits now have been forgotten or that seems the case.

What a privilege to have been born then such a long time ago.
Plus being taught to honor others' feelings was good to know.
Children were loved and emphasis on the value of kind deeds.
It was a time God and family and country filled all the needs.

Elaine Long

I FOLLOW IN FOOTSTEPS DESIGNED FOR ME

I cook because of the memories I have of a very good cook.
Also I love dearly due to the love of ones who wrote the book.
A desire to help others was taught and shown along my way.
The tender heart and soft feelings were gifts on my birth day.

Much honor and pride were taught in the course of every day.
A kind and compassionate heart was built well in order to stay.
The temper of considerable size was not left out it is so true.
I try to control it most of the time and keep it hidden deep too.

If my temperament is good or bad, at birth it was instilled in me.
In and how I was reared made me what I have now come to be.
By growing up in poverty as it would be described in print today.
The Lord knew we would be rich in beliefs so He paved my way.

I follow in the footsteps designed for me by His grace long ago.
It has become my inheritance and it goes everywhere I may go.
The family He gave me provided love and integrity of much worth.
My environment was where kindness was a signature on the earth.

Given the love of nature and soil and fellowman is a gracious gift.
The know how to enjoy the fruit of these things allows such a lift.
Parents were teachers in the safety of things requiring expertise.
Honesty was a truly a virtue so we had little need for many keys.

I have no heir to follow in my footsteps or to inherit these traits.
All of my remaining relatives were fed from the same loving plate.
God doesn't make errors and He made our family good and strong.
Now others can benefit from this gift as I pass these virtues along.

Thinking of the kind thoughtful deeds I grew up seeing in my days.
I believe this imprint I knew should be sent on in some other ways.
Using my time I will try to live the examples that were set for me.
I ask God to guide my footsteps making me a blessing to all I see.

So Much in Awe

I have priceless riches in my family and friends galore.
Their love and much concern for me I can't ever ignore.
If they are not calling they are coming by to check on me.
With such sweet loving folks I'm as blessed as I can be.

I never had this much consideration toward me before.
Till now family members kept it behind their heart's door.
I feel I am really honored and lucky and very much in awe.
Their thoughtfulness toward me beats anything I ever saw.

Any return of favor I could give isn't worth much to me.
For touching and helping or pushing or pulling you see.
My meager assistance I give to others is really quite small.
Friends and family are what is important and worth it all.

Yes it is true I enjoy and appreciate their wonderful touch.
I love each and every one and care about them very much.
Though I adore them, it can't fill the emptiness I've known.
The end of the day comes, and then I will go home all alone.

Now I'm not complaining or being mournful and real sad.
I'm only remembering the vast treasure of love I once had.
But life goes on and family now tries for me to compensate.
I'm thankful for their love and all the attention is just great.

It's sweet and nice to be thought of and loved and that is fine.
I am not sure I'm worth the trouble or so much of their time.
Any ability I use to aid someone in their time of want or need.
It comes from God and He allows me to do some small deed.

MEMORIES OF CHILDHOOD

In thoughts, I wander away to a place where I was born.
Far back, it goes to another day on a bright October morn.
It was out in the country, to a quiet place down on the farm.
Long before street drugs or violence caused anyone harm.

The lessons built integrity, respect and some common sense.
Growing crops and livestock and avoiding that barbwire fence.
Quite often there was hard work to be done, but we survived it.
Facing the difficulty made us stronger and learning not to quit.

We did not ever have much money around our house to be sure.
Yet, the love was priceless and plenty for everything to endure.
One does not need to have wealth and so many material things.
Love and honor is what is needed to be rich as a queen and king.

My life has been better due to my upbringing and strong foundation.
To ever do the bad stuff or get into trouble really held no fascination.
Attaining values, manners, and doing kind deeds was a way of life.
Those thoughtful role models I had, helped me to be a better wife.

Into each life, some rain must fall and ours certainly was the same.
We endured it and grew stronger because of our good family name.
Though one's roots does not always make a person grow up right.
The quality of childhood rearing is what really destines one's plight.

I am so proud of where I came from and what I have come to be.
For all I am, simply came from my good family education you see.
If I have helped someone's way or lightened a load then I know.
It is only passing on to others what I was taught a long time ago.

Elaine Long

THE COMMUNITY

A community is where everyone is always greeted by their first name.
All of the children acquire skills found in vacation bible school fame.
Taking for granted the love, safety and genuinely being cared about.
Children grow up emotionally and spiritually secure without a doubt.

Being welcome not only in the church family but in a neighbor's as well.
Enjoying a sense of being at home and that feeling is just simply swell.
Growing up in a little church and surrounded by a community setting.
A warm memory of the fellowship is so sweet no one will be forgetting.

The Sunday school teacher's names and their faces still remain so clear.
All the value of their teachings and influence has continued to stay near.
The warmth and guidance of the community bestowed on a small child.
It has become entwined deep in the heart and will not ever go out of style.

A neighborhood that had time to help anyone in need or was suffering so.
This gesture from the heart is a memory that has always left a cozy glow.
Such precious recollections like this are gently stored in a memory bank.
Those people's influence and inspiration on one's life has many thanks.

"Love one another," for the most part seemed to be the community goal.
Remembering that unique sensation is perfect and it has never grown old.
It seemed that our little country community may have had an extra twist.
In addition to the good people who resided there, God walked in our midst.

FRIENDS: GOD'S GIFTS

GOD'S ANGELS

A girl's most secret weapon is in the love of a true friend.
One who has a heart of gold and is there beyond the end.
No two friends ever hold the same place inside the heart.
So each friend to one's life always holds such a sweet part.

Some will listen, others guide, and protect, yet all do inspire.
Though their love is worth a fortune, yet it is not ever for hire.
Friends add color and the warmth and peace inside our life.
They are the most important one to call in the midst of strife.

Special connections are from each friend and are such a bond.
It is a feeling of being needed and belonging that I am so fond.
The soul touching silences allows our hearts to link up together.
The comfort and contentment and relief rest light as a feather.

It is the complete freedom to express unashamedly inner fears.
Even if those words are accompanied by the presence of tears.
Friends don't judge, or pry, or even try to make everything ok.
It is a comfortable and soothing sensation there on every day.

We walk hand in hand and heart to heart all along life's trail.
It is in knowing that this true token of friendship will never fail.
Meeting dates with friends are written on the calendar in ink.
For time spent with special friends helps one's ability to think.

The best friends are God's special angels He sends them near.
They have an ability to take care of everything and remove fear.
God sees and hears all and He directs angels to guide our way.
Without Him as our very best friend our life would not be okay.

ANGELS

Sometimes one can see the actions some angels bring or give.
Each loving deed and touches from their hearts forever lives.
Many a time and day, this unique love has gotten me through.
Without all the assistance, I cannot imagine what I would do.

My family and others were great and helped me so very much.
These deeds and the support and caring held an angelic touch.
Words cannot describe what the compassion has meant to me.
A love given during this time enabled some pain to run and flee.

I am so thankful God saw it best to lend those special ones to me.
So dear will these angels forever be in my wounded heart you see.
The loving mind sent from God really touched my heart and soul.
To explain or relate the tenderness that was extended can't be told.

The flutter of the angel wings was and is a peaceful, soothing sound.
Those angels, which were sent my way, wore halos or was it crowns?
Only those sent by God would know what to say and just what to do.
My life was made livable by these angelic ones sent to see me through.

The peaceful and quiet, soothing words slowly helped my heart to heal.
Through a portion of life that even now often does not seem to be real.
Any indebtedness to repay honor to this sweet kindness cannot be met.
Nevertheless, I will spend the rest of my days trying to repay this debt.

The amount of love I have received will always keep me in total awe.
For this was the most endearing display of kind sensitivity I ever saw.
Only God could have given so much love deep inside those dear hearts.
I can only hope of these wonderful, caring minds I will always be a part.

Elaine Long

PLAY ON MISS RUTH

The day is dark and cloudy and filled with a weeping rain.
It is a sad time here today and we are all in so much pain.
The news would have turned a sunny day into a dark night.
A lifelong friend left us today and it just does not feel right.

Her name was Ruth and she was both a jewel and a gem.
She had such a sharp mind even with pain and stiff limbs.
A historian she was for she could set the record straight.
I often called her with a community matter to investigate.

Over the years and subjects our minds and voices would go.
She had forgotten more than most people would ever know.
Now today she walks and talks to all of those long ago souls.
The best part is she isn't in pain and she will never grow old.

Can't you see her there meeting and greeting friend and kin?
Rejoicing with all and catching up on the many years again.
Heaven has trumpets and harps and other wonderful sounds.
I really hope it has a piano for Miss Ruth somewhere around.

So she can play once more with fingers that now freely bend.
Playing for angels' choirs and the music will never have to end.
When God called her name she left without a backward look.
She entered into Heaven and then her Master's hand she took.

Play on Miss Ruth, and play loud so once more we can hear.
Though you are in paradise I think you are still close and near.
Ask our old community crowd to start assembling at the gate.
Not many of us are left here, so they won't have long to wait.

Tell them you saw us and our message is we are on our way.
It won't be long before we can all be gathered together one day.
We miss her here on earth, but Heaven missed her much more.
The celebration began when Miss Ruth walked in Heaven's door.

Thank you Lord, for letting us have had her for all of those years.
We were blessed with that time, even though now we are in tears.
Thank you for all the lives she touched in the time she spent here.
Goodbye Miss Ruth till we meet again, you will always remain dear.

Elaine Long

Special Friends

The invitation was for a big party for two eighty year old dears.
It was so unique and wonderful it simply brought some tears.
Some long ago special friends were seen again at long last.
Neighbors and friends reminded me of good times of the past.

Some sweet memories came flooding back from way back then.
For an afternoon it became possible to go back home once again.
Familiar faces around from other times and so many happy days.
It was terrific to see each one warmly greeted like the sun's rays.

Good memories mingled with reminders of those no longer here.
Yet sometimes it seemed as if their voices one could almost hear.
In the company of this group for years has been a great experience.
Future life patterns were shaped as was good old common sense.

Life was much simpler way back then and seemed like more fun.
Even with less money somehow it was easier to get things done.
Seeing long time friends and their families was definitely pure joy.
But putting faces with names required many brain cells to employ.

Parents now with grown children of their own once sat upon my lap.
This reminds me of how many years have passed with a reality slap.
This couple with birthdays came into our lives fifty plus years ago.
God always has a reason and this is one of his blessings I know.

Some friends are as special as family and are a part of the heart.
Time spent with them will always be remembered as the best part.
A lovely time was had as good friends visited together once more.
Celebrating these sweet dears will be a good memory forevermore.

The birthday couple was at the center of everyone's attention.
Their good deeds and attributes are much too many to mention.
Except to say they are and have been always loved by everyone.
It is an honor to say, thank you dear friends for all you have done.

Golden Friendship

It really started a very long time ago back in our past.
Even so all of the time seems to have gone by so fast.
We were just teenagers on the day when we first met.
Yet soon to find us together was usually one safe bet.

After graduations we each took desk jobs downtown.
Best friends we became as we made all of our rounds.
Socializing and commuting together we became a pair.
Then later some second jobs together we would share.

I was the maid of honor for her and then she was mine.
The friendship grew and then became something fine.
Our kind husbands enjoyed our friendship benefits too.
They did not grumble when there were fun things to do.

A job change separated us with hundreds of miles apart.
But our friendship still remained deep inside each heart.
Trouble came and went but our friendship didn't waver.
A closer move came, then frequent visits we could saver.

It was wonderful to be able to see each other often again.
Daily occurrences were better shared with a best friend.
Life was good and kind for a while and was mostly well.
Changes and moves gave more pain than words can tell.

Yet friendship grew; regardless of all the miles between.
Each reunion was as sweet as some greeting card scene.
Years passed finally and it was a welcome home to stay.
Travels were over and pop in visits were possible any day.

Age and miles have taken a toll except on our friendship.
Our best friend status is strong and well and will not slip.
The reason I know it will remain, it is easy to tell or show.
This year we celebrate fifty years of friendship, so I know.

Elaine Long

ALWAYS REMEMBER

The day by day events continue to mount up high.
Irritating problems or people makes tempers fly.
Limitations or obstacles constantly block the way.
Many things make one need to vent about the day.

Don't think of it as complaining, cranky or whining.
It is to another you are relating and comfort finding.
There is a lot more room outside the body for things.
You will feel better if you give problems some wings.

Saying them out loud sometimes removes their clout.
Calling a friend will always make things better no doubt.
Especially if it is a loving friend who listens really good.
A pal who hears yet remembers only what they should.

Never consider it to be complaining or fussing too much.
Always remember reach out and a friend you will touch.
Everyone can have a bad day now and then this is true.
Times and events get one down and makes them blue.

Yet God knew this day would happen a long time ago.
Another of God's gifts is amazing friends to love us so.
It does not matter whether the sun shines on any day.
Remember special friends are near to help in any way.

ALL THOSE YEARS

I can only wonder how many times your life has crossed mine?
There were places where both of us would go to shop or dine.
Our area of travel was similar or the same in so many ways.
How often did we look at each other and on how many days?

No concept of how many miles together we then nearly walked.
It wasn't time, or the situation wasn't right to listen and to talk.
The sharing of grief or doubling of joy merely was not so near.
It was to be yet a while until grief in our hearts we would hear.

At how many functions did we maybe look in each other's eyes?
Unaware and not know or notice, one fine friendship to realize?
Could it have been at a restaurant or in some store at the mall?
Or maybe looking eye to eye while passing the other in a hall?

It was not by any ordinary chance or some unusual moon sign.
All of our needs were met by God in time and by His own design.
He guided or led our steps to each other's understanding to find.
Only by His divine connection, could one heart to the other bind.

In so many of those years we could have been very good friends.
But there was some reason we didn't know the other back then.
Situations then put us together and caused the friendship to grow.
God gave me wisdom to depend on your help more than you know.

You may have thought I was being kind but it was not quite true.
But I who needed your knowledge to do the grief steps I had to do.
The endless days and longer nights was beginning to take a toll.
Then God sent His angel to keep my life from lingering on hold.

This friendship is precious and wonderful and quite cherished too.
Forever will I be humbled and so grateful that He sent me to you.
I thank God for having allowed our lives to come together one day.
This miracle of His blessing cannot be explained any other way.

Elaine Long

THICKER THAN WATER

An old adage is, "blood is thicker than water"; meaning family ties.
This is truer than most people will ever know or be able to realize.
It happened as times were tough or loads much too heavy to bear.
The family would step right up and look after one with great care.

No matter how bleak the view or the situation, the family was near.
Family was for help and support and most of all chasing away fear.
Down through the years as I recall that was the way things went.
Helping each other by any means even down to the last red cent.

Occasionally the blood may have been thinned by endless tears.
Especially if trouble and heartache lasted on for so many years.
I am glad that I grew up in a time to be a witness to this true fact.
Now I am old and tired and families now do not know how to act.

Somewhere along the way a fantastic discovery has been made.
This blood to water theory isn't always true anymore I am afraid.
Don't despair for it is a much better thing to witness, feel and see.
Some friends are closer than a collection of family could ever be.

Their hearts are of gold with true compassion felt and very sweet.
Pure joy of true friendship makes one's life happy and complete.
The love of a wonderful friend is more priceless than any pearls.
It resembles a huge beacon of love and lights up life and the world.

One doesn't have to have blood connections to be part of the family.
It is a wonderful blessing and a special treasure and will always be.
A touch of Heaven is felt in each smile, hug and at every meeting.
A refreshing touch for the heart and it is renewed at every greeting.

She Seemed to Understand

I thought I had walked through the darkest of midnight.
But then I wasn't walking all alone in the midst of fright.
No matter how hard it was to face yet another tomorrow.
Her little tongue would try to lick away the tears of sorrow.

Brittany understood me more than I gave to her the credit.
She tried to divert my attention and hoped I might forget it.
She sensed when I was sad and would come offer her paw.
Without any doubt, she was the sweetest dog I ever saw.

If I was sick or having a real tough time trying to breathe.
She would sit near by and watch me until my panic eased.
She is now in Heaven and for the first time now I am alone.
The only company I now have comes by way of the phone.

Oh, I knew I would miss Brittany when her time was through.
Even while seeing or talking to her and hearing her move too.
I had no idea all of my loneliness would come flooding back.
Or that it would gather momentum to strike like a battle attack.

All the ten years she blessed our home with her faithful love.
That loyalty cannot be measured in words except from above.
She and I came into each other's lives for a reason back then.
Then we lost my soul mate and Brittany became a close friend.

I never had to try to keep my composure when in front of her.
She didn't even mind when I held her and cried into her soft fur.
Dear Brittany became everyone's loving, little sweetie I know.
Yet she loved me completely and followed wherever I would go.

There was such dedication and total devotion she held for me.
Another dog may come but never another Brittany will I see.
A mark she left on my heart and on all who ever came her way.
She taught all of us how to show more love to others every day.

Elaine Long

EVERYONE IS SMILEY WITH RILEY

People may be tired or in pain when they come in at my door.
But, all of those feelings or tension will soon fade into the floor.
My new dog now enjoying the life of Riley is a bouncing little boy.
He had a purpose for being sent here and is such a bundle of joy.
His ever-changing cute antics bring much laughter to everyone.
Rotten is all about loving you first and then having so much fun.

I called Brittany my little shadow; she was always a constant pal.
She followed everywhere I went and was truly my wonderful gal.
Riley is my new scout or the fearless leader and runs far ahead.
He tries to do, see and smell all and be the first but not ever led.
His favorite thing to do is to race over and leap up into my chair.
He lays his head on my chair arm, as if he has always been there.

If I do not make him get up, he will turn over and lay on his back.
Then with his four feet in the air, modesty he does seem to lack.
Riley sleeps this way for hours then slowly rolls down to the floor.
He then grabs a toy and plays or hides a treat behind every door.
This rascal likes to touch someone as he listens or when he sleeps.
It is not unusual for him to come and lay down on both of one's feet.

Yet, it is hard to keep from smiling when this new doggy is around.
He craves attention, hugs, pats, and acts as if he is one silly clown.
He does not meet any strangers and is always ready for a van ride.
So as not to miss a view, he runs and looks out from side to side.
Mr. Ham always wants to be seen and noticed everywhere we go.
From the back seat in a drive thru, he puts his head out to say hello.

It brings a smile to the face in the window then O'Riley smiles too.
At the pet store, he shows off by choosing his own toy as if on cue.
With his personality, he could be a good will ambassador for all.
The frowns would fade and attitudes soften if Sir Riley was on call.
I miss the Brittany I had so many years and I guess I always will.
Often I will call Brittany's name when talking or calling to Riley still.

Brittany would not have tolerated any other dog or even any mention.
She was jealous of me, and wanted and received all of my attention.
The Lord had Riley waiting in the wings until it was just the right time.
He took our Brittany home and then sent Riles on his way to be mine.
I think she must have sent Smiley a note or had some contact with him.
He has some of her attributes and reminders and that makes him a gem.

Elaine Long

THE MOST BEAUTIFUL GIFT

A birthday thankfully just adds numbers but once a year.
Then it is only one time a season when Christmas is near.
Adults are relieved these yearly events only come once.
It is so much rushing and too many goodies to munch.

I guess I am special or maybe more blessed than most.
For all year I have my loved ones and family very close.
To me it means Christmas and birthdays are each day.
Their presence is a wonderful present to me in all ways.

My birthday gifts are great and come in every smile.
Christmas presents are in each hug and last a while.
Endless love comes from my sweet family and friends.
It is continuous and has not a beginning or any end.

Do not go shopping for me for birthday or Christmas fare.
It is quite simply the warmth of your love I want to share.
No other thing means more than your friendship to me.
Your company in my life makes it worth living you see.

Now put a smile on your face and a hug inside your heart.
And know I have had the most beautiful gift from the start.
This friendship simply grows more perfect in every way.
The size and color are fine, enjoyed and adored each day.

TEARS OF GRIEF

A LINGERING FAREWELL

When a much loved person suddenly dies and goes home.
One is left in shock and disbelief from becoming all alone.
The unexpected death is most traumatic to say the least.
Raw feelings are with such anger at the ugly death beast.

A death unprepared for just simply takes one's breath away.
Nothing or no one can ever remove all the pain from that day.
Other times a terminal illness allows the sad family to know.
Never ready to give up, but it is less of a shock when they go.

Some people wear out and it is a quiet serenity when they die.
Their quality of life was badly diminished often they would cry.
Another had Alzheimer's; their mind completely disappeared.
Long before death they couldn't recognize the kids they reared.

Another one is a lingering farewell that is really hard to explain.
This one hurts for many years and little can describe the pain.
Problems follow setbacks; then diseases in multiples appear.
Though uncertain when, one knows the death is looming near.

The only goal or aim a spouse has is to make each day superb.
Remaining positive yet comforting with any cross words unheard.
The tears and suffering keep appearing unexpectedly in each day.
Praying hard yet knowing time is short and he will be going away.

Day to month and for years, terror gripes the heart hard and fast.
Stress and emotion on the nerves tighten as death comes at last.
Heartache and pain have been felt long before breathing ceases.
A final curtain falls and fear and reality turn the heart into pieces.

Death or a loss of love is not easy whatever the situation may be.
It may take beyond forever for any reason for one's death to see.
A comfortable thing is God's strength through pain and the grief.
The comfort He gives or causes will always bring the most relief.

The Day Someone Dies

When one dies, for those left behind it is a day from hell.
Truthfully that will not be the worst day, I can soulfully tell.
The mournful day a loved one dies is only the opening act.
Before sanity returns one will wish for death it is a sad fact.

The worst days by far will be the ones to live through alone.
Such loneliness is indescribable with the loved one gone.
The events of that sad day have changed life for evermore.
Those who walked this way know the misery yet in store.

On the death day, people come to help and assist and aid.
Hovering around, staying busy until all the respects are paid.
The next days are filled with schedules and tasks and friends.
But when the events are over and the painful reality sets in.

Before the silence so deafening is over, one will wish for a day.
To be filled with happy things and not obstacles all the way.
The mind can only dread and feel the dreadful hurt for so long.
One never forgets, but after time the pain will be less, not gone.

There will always be a scar, an inner ache and a real need.
The memory lives forever but the hurt in time does recede.
Life goes on for those around and one must go with the flow.
However, a reminder causes a wince no one else can know.

Elaine Long

THE ANGUISH OF THE MIND

Until one that is tied to your heart dies, you can't know.
How it affects the fiber of your being from head to toe.
You can't understand how it feels to say a last goodbye.
Or just how quickly those memories can make you cry.

The emptiness of being alone may dull but never leaves.
The stark reality of it will make one buckle at the knees.
A home is a journal of memories made together to adore.
Special moments come into view by the opening of a door.

Some days are easy but some take an abundance of nerve.
The vacant place in your life a reminder forever will serve.
The loss of one tied to the heart will cut and stab and slice.
Only with God will you have faith enough to pay the price.

The greater the price one pays for faith the stronger it grows.
That takes much time to realize and then only you will know.
It is like life has a way of putting faith and strength to a test.
But at those times you will surely wonder if God knows best.

The anguish of the mind will make you be both sad and weak.
There will be days words won't come and others you will speak.
You may think your heart will stop by being overcome by grief.
All of your body will ache badly and nothing will bring any relief.

You do not get over the loss of one who made your heart throb.
Yet you will learn how to function and adjust without many sobs.
Inside you will be screaming hoping and praying to go insane.
It is very possible to know then you will never again be the same.

Guilt will rise when new experiences you have do not include them.
Pain will wax and wane yet will never end but it will only grow dim.
You cannot change the past, nor alone expect to mend your heart.
God will help and heal and give you peace if you let Him do his part.

God created our minds so questioning things and asking why is ok.
He doesn't get upset with us no matter what we may think or say.
God has known grief much greater than anything that we ever can.
He knows the reason to everything and controls it all with His hand.

Elaine Long

MEMORIES: HEAVEN OR HELL

Memories can be like Heaven or they can come from hell.
Sometimes the same memory can be from both as well.
By recalling a warm musing shall at times soothe the soul.
Other reminders on rainy days will make one feel so old.

Anniversaries or notable days can sure bring on some pain.
Most especially when the one involved won't be seen again.
Life seems to be all about learning just how to say goodbye.
Why can pleasure or sorrow be relieved some by a good cry?

All love and pain, just like happiness and sadness is a pair.
For each one can't be felt without so many emotions there.
One can have pain without experiencing love it is very true.
Having love without knowing some pain is impossible to do.

Pain is immeasurable when a death one's world does destroy.
Nevertheless life would be a sad world without love to enjoy.
"It is better to have loved and lost than not have loved at all."
It is true but doesn't help when all alone or talking to a wall.

It makes no sense standing in a cemetery talking to a stone.
Realizing all that was experienced together is now long gone.
All one can hope for is finally reaching a day where pain is dead.
The precious memories of love forever will remain in the head.

A reason for everything and one is found in some memories too.
Whether a good or bad one, or maybe a painful memory or two.
One simply has a deep feeling that some things were meant to be.
God will allow peace and comfort on the remainder of life for me.

No Matter the Reason

A faint smile but the longing for my beloved is concealed.
The sad thoughts and lonely feelings in the heart are sealed.
On the outside a smile may seemingly be without one care.
Yet the inside reveals a big frown that is so full of despair.

To most, love and joy and laughter are faked with the eyes.
Only to keep from revealing the sadness that still inside lies.
Thoughts of him, like a melody, heard yet impossible to see.
The music of his soft voice is now only just a faded memory.

An imaginary chest holds favorite treasures of a long time ago.
Some are painful, sweet, or sad, but all too endearing to let go.
They are always just outside my grasp of reaching out to touch.
The memories do not hold a candle to the one I love so much.

Life seems to go on for everyone else except sometimes for me.
Somehow I don't think I will live long enough for my pain to flee.
The ache, loneliness, and endless void are pressing on my heart.
Though the years are moving on, this pain does not want to part.

Tears are always right below the surface just waiting for their time.
Some days tears seem to fall without having any reason or rhyme.
Maybe I am feeling sorry for myself or so lonesome on those days.
Could it be some delayed emotions inside finally finding its way?

No matter what, so much pain seems to remain deep down inside.
So now and then when it crosses over a nerve, I just want to hide.
The real simple words will sometimes find their way out of my pen.
It cannot completely describe all the turmoil that still resides within.

Elaine Long

WORDS CAN'T DESCRIBE

Can one ever begin to describe the feeling of a great loss?
Does a word exist in the dictionary that measures all the cost?
No, to each one it would be a different expression of so much.
One's description to another's perception would not ever touch.

For me the severe ache was surpassed only by a persistent fear.
I often asked my heart, "Oh how can I live without him near?"
All of those long and lonely hours stretched out end to end.
They are so painful despite the help of family and dear friends.

I have whys and how's in my mind that only a few ever knew.
Then with stark realization of what would I ever be able to do?
At one time, each day was agony beyond any comprehension.
Looking back all my life existed on then was very much tension.

Eons of time thought to be so painfully slow did finally move on.
Step by step, I began to exist again, yet not living with him gone.
Now much later the pain in my heart has grown somewhat numb.
To many that probably will sound so stupid and even quite dumb.

It is as though the heart wound has had all of the nerves removed.
The scars remain, but the severe pain is now somewhat subdued.
My loss will always be deeply felt and that world so greatly missed.
Life will go on; yet many things I once did, I will no longer risk.

The tears have nearly dried and skies are looking some brighter.
Now I sure hold on to all my dear memories a whole lot tighter.
I will never again be the same but the ache has dulled and faded.
Being a widow will always be a label to be despised and hated.

The numbness or empty or hollow sensations are so very real.
Each is a deep emotion this death forced me to painfully feel.
My life goes on but not as well as before and the void is great.
That is just how it is and feels when one has lost their mate.

Life does not always turn out fair but then who said it should?
Jesus probably thought that too when at the cross He stood.
All things on earth are for a reason whether bad, good or sad.
God is in control of all the earth and that makes me so glad.

Elaine Long

THE FORCE AND STRENGTH OF THUNDER

My deep wounds are hidden behind the face I wear.
It is the loss of my great love that has put them there.
Only the wonderful memories of him can I hold still.
Now all stored safely in my heart and they always will.

My painful scars go much deeper than anyone knows.
The book of love made on our journey will never close.
I wish I could leave all the dark shadows of life behind.
But with this heart quake; true peace may not be mine.

Any death leaves a hole in a life that can never be filled.
It doesn't matter how many years ago, it still is not real.
All I have left is a shrine of love for him inside my heart.
Even walking in and around all he made is a hard part.

Others can't see, feel or know the depth of such sorrow.
My heartbreaking loss is always there in every tomorrow.
The intense pain has the force and strength of thunder.
My life was torn apart from within and flung all asunder.

God made all of the mountains and valleys of our life too.
He knew how much each one of us had to walk through.
It is never more than one can undertake or withstand.
That's a comfort and helpful but I miss that sweet man.

The storm cloud of my emptiness maybe will end one day.
A breaking of dawn may chase some of the shadows away.
The sun will shine again one day and my path will be clear.
No matter where it leads, God will always be near and dear.

THE BITTER JOURNEY

The death of a loved one is a life changing event.
One's heart and hope is shattered, broken or bent.
No answers for the pain that rages around inside.
Or why all the prayers offered, failed and they died.

Many problems left unanswered and so many whys.
"Why didn't God intervene and just not let them die?"
Understanding why one died or prayers did not work.
Why doctors didn't help why, one could go berserk.

One could doubt God and man and be mad at all of them.
Honest feelings shake one's soul and the reliance in Him.
People are in shock and disbelief that God didn't prevail.
In times like these loyalty is shaken or it may even fail.

Confusion is always a constant companion in every way.
Much anger and disappointment seem to abound each day.
Survive each day and then finally able to allow forgiving.
Life will again go on but the optional part will be the living.

The question is not if one will move on but it will be when.
Nothing can ever be the same or anything like it was again.
But as time moves on, one of two things will happen for sure.
The realization of with trust in God anything one can endure.

Ability will come to move on with a deeper faith for all seasons.
Or else one will lose or doubt their faith in God and the reasons.
One has to find what brings comfort and answers and peace.
Each one is different, yet the bitter journey of grief can cease.

ONLY TIME WILL TELL

The sun rises today like always and as it will continue to do.
An entire world goes on their way as usual on this day too.
The birds are flying busily along with some mission in mind.
Everything is good except for me and my day is blue I find.

Where the sadness and pain comes from I haven't got a clue.
I only know that ever so often my day turns a deep dark blue.
Too many memories seem to be waiting around every bend.
They all remind me that the hole in my heart will never mend.

That old saying that, "time heals all wounds", is simply not right.
Some hurts are here to stay and actually ache more late at night.
A saying of, "an absence makes the heart grow fonder" is so true.
For there are days a big heavy cloud hangs over everything I do.

It is really impossible to explain the feeling that comes over me.
It is for the most part without any particular reason that I can see.
Just when I think I am ok and with living my life alone I can cope.
Then that old sad mood overtakes me and I simply lose my hope.

I wonder if these sad weepy days will ever end and be no more.
Will it ever be possible to finally close that old memories door?
Or will it remain open till my death finally lays this burden down?
I pray for some relief to come from the pain to which I am bound.

Only time will tell if the blue days will ever no longer to me appear.
Until then I can hope and pray those sad days will finally disappear.
More memories or less could be the key to finally closing that door.
Yet I suspect either way those blue days will be felt for evermore.

THAT IS WHAT THEY SAY

Have you ever been faced with an aching, broken heart?
Did you know if you had a future or even how to start?
Have you looked at a sunrise and could only see gray?
Did you panic when the sorrow took your breath away?

If you have stayed awake often long into many a night.
Did you wonder if you would cry past the morning light?
If you turned away to hide the tears; words not able to say.
Or felt so much anguish deep within your heart each day.

If you have had to say goodbye to one you loved so dear.
Did you worry if you could withstand all the flood of fear?
If you thought this death would make you lose your mind.
Yet also thinking it might be better than being left behind.

Have you ever felt alone and lonely in a people filled room?
So all you could do was wish that it would be over real soon.
If you know there is a Heaven for you have walked thru Hell,
Yet by surviving it with not only faith but some hope as well.

Then friend you too have left your aching heart beside a grave.
You also doubted if you would have the courage to be brave.
Battle scarred and so weary, now lost in grief and worry worn.
Life wrecked and nerves shredded and a future looking forlorn.

But hour by hour to day by day the pain slightly recedes away.
Finally a light is at the end of the tunnel and makes a better day.
Time heals all wounds, or at least that is what they always say.
Yet steady faith in God and love of friends helped all the way.

Elaine Long

A Reason for Tears

Some days are so tough, and yet other days are tougher still.
Sunny days seem to go fast and the dark days just never will.
Without any warning the grief comes and covers like the dew.
It spreads some low moods and weepy thoughts all around too.

A sense is of losing restraint of feelings and those emotions.
The mind seems to have deserted me with some other notions.
Tears are impatiently waiting to surface and rage out of control.
All hope is lost of averting the teardrops or the heart to console.

Sometimes emotional and physical things are too much to bear.
The battered heart has no time or energy to take note or beware.
The overwhelming waves of panic can only add to the unrest.
It can only be dreaded exactly as though it was some bad test.

The heart is often feeling lonely and nearly full of so much gloom.
Not understanding why there is sadness in the air around the room.
However, tears are but one of God's wonderful and powerful gifts.
When enough of them have fallen down, one's heart will then lift.

The tears wash away some worry and pain and keep trouble at bay.
God will send a rainbow of dear friends at some point along the way.
Teardrops wash over the soul and clear the cobwebs from the heart.
After the tears flow, the body is refreshed and ready for a new start.

God created the ability for one to cry so it is ok, for His is the best way.
It will take many tears before it starts to wash some of the blues away.
Many times, we never know the basis, or cause, or have any reason.
Nevertheless, it is surprising when sad emotions have their season.

GRIEF DOES NOT ALWAYS WAIT

A person really can go through a lot of agony in grief.
They seek to find themselves doing anything for relief.
Some will try to temper the pain with alcohol a plenty.
Others think they can dilute pain with tears of many.

Some can smile and hold it inside behind a fake face.
Others may give up and simply run away in great haste.
A select few can handle it with dignity and some grace.
Most people get through it and yet it is too much to face.

They spend all their energy to handle grief in many ways.
Some wrongly think they are over it in about three days.
They blame the one who died but that is only an escape.
Others may get on with their life and not seem to hesitate.

Grief does not always seem to wait until someone has died.
Grief begins when the signs or diagnosis cannot be denied.
Tears may have about run out long before the sick one dies.
There is not a limit to just how much one can ultimately cry.

Nor does the grief ever end for it is always just below the skin.
It sits and waits for a wee chance to raise its ugly head again.
Each one could write a book on their rocky road through grief.
All the accounts would be true for each has to find their relief.

Only one good thing can be said about the pain of grief today.
In time hurt will end and paradise in Heaven will be a great day.
Loving someone is like a brief time spent inside a lovely paradise.
But losing a dear loved one is to pay a unimaginable painful price.

Maybe I Can Help

Today maybe I can find a way to help someone.
One who lost a lot and has such burdens to bear.
Who needs a friend to hold a hand till hurt is done.
Let me do my part to show how much I really care.

I cannot ever walk in that someone else's shoes.
I know I will not ever know their feelings as my own.
Their dear loved ones were not any of mine to lose.
I can only remember how I felt with my love gone.

Show me how to not judge or talk or even declare.
That I know just how and what they should do now.
The best I can do is to remember them often in prayer.
That will help remove weight from their troubled brow.

I can hope a word I say or with some gesture I could.
Or give them peace and strength to face another day.
And that some things aren't meant to be understood.
Most broken hearts will heal but will never go away.

Sadly some rain showers must fall into each one's life.
For rain is the pain one's life sometimes brings to bear.
Some more than others have hurt cutting like a knife.
No one knows how much rain each life has to share.

Just as flowers without rain can never begin to grow.
Then each shower helps to make one so much stronger.
After the rain has ended the birds will sing again I know.
May I find a way to help one hang on just a little bit longer.

Giving some answers to questions yet unsaid just won't do.
The pain; clouds my mind from thinking sound for a while.
I can do more by just listening to what they went through.
Now every once in a while give them a reassuring smile.

NO ONE EXCEPT GOD

Friend, I have been in the place where you now walk.
For me to say I know how you feel would be just talk.
No one except God knows exactly how you will feel.
It is only by His grace and love your sorrow can heal.

God never walks ahead of you or even close behind.
But beside you and the best friend you will ever find.
At times when your pain is great He will send someone
To give you a reassuring nod or hug as warm as the sun.

Some folks may try to tell you how you feel or should do.
These are not the ones God sends to walk you through.
They may tell you to stop acting like you are ill or sick.
And some will expect you to lose all the grief real quick.

God bless them, they mean well but have not any clue.
They have not walked the lonely road that you now do.
If you have sanity left and can say to them one and all.
"Thank you so much, if I ever need you I will just call."

Only God is your friend, and dear angels He may send.
It will be the right ones there until the grief and hurt ends.
Once again I only know what worked for me and mine.
God always works, just try prayer, and peace you will find.

Elaine Long

PERHAPS EVERYTHING IS ALRIGHT

After the death of a loved one you have to choose.
To survive and go on existing or your life you lose.
It takes so much more strength to decide to live again.
It would be easier to quit trying and just let living end.

One can proceed in going on surviving in so many ways.
It may be forcing one's self to get out of bed each day.
Or maybe it is just pretending everything is still the same.
It could be playing the being ever so tough person game.

Perhaps everything is alright and you will soon again be ok.
The bottom line is grief is a walk in hell every single day.
One is never able to really get over this thing called grief.
In time one learns to live with it and that is the only relief.

So many little things will allow one to finally get to this place.
One can't do it alone there are too many mountains to face.
Friends and family and most of all, God allow one to heal.
Yet the tender scar across the heart one will forever feel.

I CAN ONLY IMAGINE

If your feelings are hurt, I can only imagine the pain.
But I will hope you can soon feel much better again.

If you are having a real bad day, I can only imagine it.
But I will pray you will find strength to get through it.

If your faith wavers or wanes, I can only imagine why.
But I will share mine until yours returns by and by.

If you feel unloved, I can only imagine the anxiety around.
But I will offer you love until calm and peace are found.

If your heart is broken in grief, I can only imagine the ache.
But I will pray for God to soothe and heal the heartbreak.

You have my hope, wishes, faith, love, and prayers too.
Anything else for you will also be a joy and pleasure to do.

But you must forgive me, for my not telling you how you feel.
See I can only imagine your misery, when beside you I kneel.

One simply cannot feel another's burdens lying on their heart.
But to help you cope, will be an honor and privilege on my part.

As you wrestle with all of your pain, or problems, or even woe.
I can only imagine your feelings, but God is wherever you go.

THE SUN SHINES A LITTLE LESS BRIGHT

Pull down the darkest shades and turn on all the big lights.
I am doing all I can to shut out the dark days and nights.
I am retreating in a shell trying desperately my grief to hide.
Above all I did not allow anyone to see my pain as I cried.

It is quite an agonizing walk through pain on most of the days.
That heavy load of much loneliness over my heart just stays.
One never knows what they are made of down deep inside.
But a death will destroy all safety nets that are on the outside.

All of the feelings and misery cannot be addressed at one time.
It seems to continue multiplying in the heart and over the mind.
An overwhelming sense of being totally alone just takes control.
If in time it becomes bearable one will find they have grown old.

The attitude about everything changes the outlook forevermore.
All aspects of love are looked at quite differently than ever before.
I wonder if I will ever live long enough for this heart to mend.
For a place, or words or a sense of loss, it brings hurt back again.

A birthday or anniversary date will in a familiar remembered place.
It makes one's breath shorter and the damaged old heart just race.
Those dear memories of what once was make me feel so very sad.
I am not sure I realized I was so blessed then with what all I had.

A life moves forward but the living again really only will be optional.
Thinking one will ever get over a loss and forget it all is a lot of bull.
The sun shines a little less bright or warm than it was for me now.
The wind is cooler and the rainy days are much sadder somehow.

Only one thing could ever remove all of the grief, ache and pain.
It will only be seeing all those loved ones in Heaven once again.
There rain or any hurt will not exist and cannot ruin another day.
An eternity in paradise will be glorious in each and every way.

MY MISSION AND MY DESIRE

I may not have seen your pain through your eyes.
Or the full measure of your sorrow ever realize.
Yet I've seen enough grief through my own heart.
To know that loneliness is always the hardest part.

Your troubles and burdens weigh heavily on you.
Then some days are more difficult to get through.
My heart felt love is all I offer to you just now.
Lean on me if need be; my shoulder will not bow.

I am now and will ever be your most faithful friend.
Now always and forever on that you can depend.
My mission and my desire will be my greatest goal.
It is to bring comfort to you and to soothe your soul.

Elaine Long

LIFE HAS CHANGED ME

The death of a close loved one is such a horrible sad trip.
All of the grief and pain and hurt can cause a mind to slip.
One cannot travel on this journey and remain the same.
Sense of loss and heartbreak and loneliness are to blame.

One becomes much different forever and in so many ways.
So many thoughts and memories become a part of my days.
Remembering their loss is so painful; yet an honor to them.
All the love and affection felt inside will not ever grow dim.

I was much different before from what I have become now.
Life has changed me for some better, yet worse somehow.
I am more compassionate, kinder and somewhat patient too.
Yet nerves have frayed and tears are near in all I say or do.

Words can sometimes cut deep from some unknowing chatter.
A lump in my throat prevents me from telling what is the matter.
People often say things like, "move on, do things and start living."
Since they can't and don't feel my heart, I just try to be forgiving.

Surviving my life alone is what I try desperately every day to do.
I don't ever expect to get over it, for it is a life-changing event too.
A loss of one so loved is almost impossible to bear from the start.
The mom, dad, or sibling, spouse or child all are tied to the heart.

All are equally devastating to say goodbye to for ones left behind.
No one can ever measure the depth of grief resting on one's mind.
Their pain of loss is felt forever and deep within the heart it will sit.
It is possible to get beyond the grief, but one will never get over it.

Do not think of me as strange or weird or maybe something odd.
I don't expect you to feel my pain or to give an understanding nod.
Just treat me normal and don't pretend to feel or somehow know.
I can't help not being the same person after this life altering blow.

Some days are better, so maybe one day I can smile and mean it.
This life awakening event is harder for me than you from where I sit.
I will smile and participate when possible and do the very best I can.
If I don't accept or agree, let me be, even if you cannot understand.

Elaine Long

LIFE IS LIKE A MOVIE

When people ask me how I am doing, I say, "I'm fine."
It is easier to say that, than all of my feelings to define.
If I say, "I'm ok", or, "I'm fine", it's what all hope to hear.
Most do not know what else to say or want to interfere.

Everyone wants it to be over and back to like it use to be.
Frankly, no one ever wanted that nearly as much as me.
I want to roll back that calendar and start all over again.
Yet it does not work that way for all living has some pain.

Eventually everyone has his or her world turn upside down.
In those times, it is just somewhat easier to wear a frown.
Even a solemn face or tough exterior provides a nice shell.
If inner turmoil cannot be seen then I look ok and all is well.

Do not assume or judge my feelings for you have no idea.
Just be thankful if we have a visit and you do not see a tear.
I want this feeling to end much more than you will ever know.
For it is like some bulky baggage following everywhere I go.

The very best thing you can ever do for me and for you too.
Take nothing for granted and live and love each day through.
Live each day as though it was the last one here on this earth.
Try not to sweat the small stuff for in the end, it has no worth.

Life is like a movie except that it has no rewind mode or replay.
Mistakes cannot be edited out or filmed over on another day.
A stand in will not be found or a hero coming to save the day.
Life is comedy, drama, suspense, and horror it is safe to say.

An intermission does not come, only endless pain to endure.
No stage lights will dim and hide the bad stuff that is for sure.
The movie will not end and the endless misery will ruin the play.
After the final curtain call, tomorrow might not be another day.

When death takes a person, only dear memories remain to hold.
All who linger have lost their heart, mind and they will grow old.
Then life winds down and soon the ending credits began to roll.
This completes the cycle of life that God created and foretold.

HOLIDAYS AND SEASONS

A New Year

Here we are at the beginning of yet another new year.
Whatever looms ahead may be joy or sadness or fear.
For some with much sickness it may mean some sorrow.
In love it's, today more than yesterday, less than tomorrow.

The ones who are grieving now may finally find some relief.
Others who have been bad may now turn over a new leaf.
A lot of anything can be done in three hundred sixty five days.
The chances are many to change our habits or make new ways.

We have a possibility of seeing new snow on one winter morning.
Perhaps see a spectacular sunrise on a new perfect day dawning.
It is really a good thing we cannot ever see what will lay ahead.
Some things might worry us so much we would take to our bed.

Joyful events that may yet to be, we would be impatient to wait.
Relationships that may come or go would be one to yearn or hate.
So it is better if we know about only one hour or one day at a time.
We can thank our dear Lord for always to us being so very kind.

May we put faith and trust in Him to decide what is best for us.
Then whatever comes to try and remember not to worry or fuss.
The new year will not have more than we can bear or even to fear.
If we recall, our precious Lord no matter what, will always be near.

THE FOURTH OF JULY

Today has dawned so clear and sunny and bright.
The dry air and cool temperature sure feel just right.
It is a birthday celebration for the United States today.
And independence and freedom were born on this day.

The importance of this day sometimes we nearly ignore.
Yet it is always special and really means so much more.
The sacrifice and life so many gave freely for the cause.
It is for all of them we always need to kneel and to pause.

For freedom came with great cost and was not ever free.
The large price tag can never be paid for by you or me.
God's grace is good and so are our dear service friends.
Or our free expression could be in jeopardy once again.

We have brave men and women today around the earth.
Defending and guarding the value and contents and worth.
Of everything we have or need or will forever hold so dear.
Let us never be ashamed to choke up or even shed a tear.

When the old red white and blue flag is waved and raised.
We should never fail to give it much honor and due praise.
Thank you, God for the privilege of living in this great land.
Make us ever grateful for the payment given by fellow man.

IT WOULD BE NICE

Here comes September with all of its pain and woe.
Everything about this month is hurtful to me it is so.
From reminder dates or rain and things dying in the fall.
It is a sad and lonely month for me and I dislike it all.

October follows with cold and dark and leaves all falling.
The harvest time has sad memories that come a calling.
Loneliness and blue moods reign the entire month long.
It will be months yet before all the dark days will be gone.

November has sad days too with the gloom still all around.
Birthday dates and family oriented holidays gets one down.
Colder days and longer nights make for some bad days too.
Then if it should rain or snow it really makes the month blue.

December comes in decked out on colors of red and green.
Christmas is on everything and signs of ole Santa are seen.
Yet without family it is always the saddest month of them all.
That simply leaves one with no reasons to plan to deck a hall.

January arrives and brings a brand new year for one to live.
Snow and ice and cold are mostly what the month has to give.
More birthdates of the dear loved ones gone on home to stay.
This revives old memories that seem to rain on a cloudy day.

February strides in for lovers and ones with hearts all aglow.
The Valentine's Day is just for couples or it is filled with woe.
Roses and candy and jewelry shaped like the love of hearts.
It is just another lonesome day for spouses who had to part.

So those six months of the year for me are blue and so bad.
Too many reminders of people no longer here make me sad.
It would be nice to hibernate for those six months of the year.
Then the rest of the year I wouldn't have so much pain or fear.

I Can Pretend

The sky is turning darker with the clouds closing in.
It looks like it will be one more day from hell again.
Day after day the bleak clouds have blocked the sun.
Overcast and dreary and depressing is not any fun.

Lord forgive me, you know best when we need rain.
But a rain filled gloomy day causes distress and pain.
The sun is concealed and cannot show its bright face.
Lord could you send a rainbow to brighten the place?

There I go again Lord, all in your business of what to do.
Instead of thanking you for Fall being lush and green too.
Grant patience to endure and walk with me all day through.
For all these miserable and overcast days make me blue.

Fall, to me was already the saddest part of the entire year.
Leaves falling and days shorter, the dying season is near.
Fall is in the air and the grip of summer has lost its touch.
The sad silence remains and shatters the nerves so much.

The harvest season is here and the cycle of life is done.
It is a completion of growing and living time under the sun.
The complexity of the phases of the moon is God's creation.
Everything is born, lives, and then dies, without explanation.

The majority of the world will continue along their merry way.
Only the lonesome ones feel like hiding on each dismal day.
My hope and prayer is, tomorrow the sun will again shine.
If it does, then I can simply pretend everything is just fine.

ALL HOLIDAYS ARE SO LONELY

Dear Lord, make me remember you are just a prayer away.
Thanks to you it is the only way I can get through each day.
Thanksgiving comes and I'm most thankful when it has gone.
It is only one of the saddest times that I have lived or known.

Before I can regroup, then Christmas is rounding the bend.
Oh, when will these painful holidays ever come to an end?
All holidays are so lonely, Lord even when I try my very best.
Getting past these days is simply a great struggle and big test.

It is impossible to celebrate or be happy on any of these days.
A heavy load of sadness upon my heart just forever weighs.
All holidays are hard to endure for I know how much I miss.
The gift I would treasure the most would be a hug and kiss.

Yet I know I never again will have it or that tender loving touch.
Though I cannot hold him, I will always love him so very much.
A new year looms in the future and it's just another pain to face.
I am forever alone and lonesome and always feel out of place.

It is still so hard even after all of a million or so painful years.
As the pain and sadness mix together, they always cause tears.
Home or not it seems to be impossible to make the pain go away.
Yet I keep hoping and praying that it will finally happen one day.

Lord, forgive me for being weak when I should stand up so strong.
My prayer is and shall be Lord, to ever be with me as I walk along.
Help me to push the clouds of sadness aside and look for better days.
I pray for strength to be able to finally see some of sunshine's rays.

CHRISTMAS SPIRIT

Christmas is no longer about the trees, the sparkle or trim,
Or shopping for the perfect gift to accommodate a whim.
The season no longer holds all the magic and surprise.
The spirit loses more of its joy each time someone dies.

Lost is the desire to get everything done and have it right.
The work and effort is not needed on Christmas Eve night.
The simplest things around Christmas now mean the most.
It is all about family and friends to love; than doing the most.

Cherished memories of all Christmas' past are packed away.
Ornaments and decorations do not the season make today.
A warm greeting and a lingering hug granted from the heart.
These are more precious than any gift of gold could impart.

The material things, not important; only love and life are now.
Together we will make it through the sad season somehow.
Holidays are simpler now unlike cherished ones from the past.
The Christmas spirit is a heart thing yet it does not forever last.

Counting the empty chairs at the table will cause one to mourn.
As well as the quiet, empty moments early on Christmas morn.
Yet nothing here could change those circumstances in any way.
The loved ones gone on would not want us to be sad on this day.

The older I get the more important things in life I can clearer see.
Seeing others happy and loved allows much satisfaction for me.
The many warm thoughts I've stored will last until I am quite old.
I am very thankful for having those memories to have and hold.

May we put our sad thoughts and tears aside and raise our glass.
To all the good times we had and all the loved ones in our past.
Then tip the glass to all our loves who are now celebrating above.
Let's make a toast to our adored here today we hold close in love.

Elaine Long

It Is Most Unusual

I just gave into some feelings of deep hurt this day.
To stop or try to control it there just was not any way.
I am still in shock that I allowed my feelings to show.
I normally keep emotions concealed everywhere I go.

My feelings have always been worn out on my sleeve.
Being hurt often, not letting one know is how I believed.
I felt if no one ever got to see just how really soft I am.
No one could take advantage of it or get me into a jam.

It is most unusual for anyone to ever get to see my tears.
Being seen as so tender hearted is what I always feared.
That is why I always wear a somewhat tough exterior shell.
So I will not get my feelings hurt badly and feel sad as well.

But today I could not hold back and the tears freely rolled.
It ruined the entire day and my future outlook took a toll.
Maybe it is because it is coming to the fall season of the year.
I hate fall and all it brings with sad days ahead and so near.

Maybe from September to March I should just go hibernate.
Become like a mean old bear and sleep out all those dates.
Getting old and ornery is certainly not the way to have fun.
I wonder how much worse it will get before my life is done?

Embarrassed and appalled that my composure I lost a hold.
Being calm and quietly in charge of me is my everyday goal.
The events of the future are a painful chore I hope to endure.
I certainly trust my present hurt will find itself a complete cure.

Maybe for the remaining time I have left to live upon this earth.
I should wear all my feelings inside and just forget their worth.
If I would turn hard and cold and uncaring and just plain mean.
No one will care for me then though my feelings won't be seen.

IT IS ANOTHER RAINY DAY

If I did not know better it would seem
      as if everyone in heaven is crying.
I know it is not true, it is just the amount
      of raindrops to which I am referring.

There is not much difference in raindrops or
      teardrops, they both appear and fall.
Rainy and dark overcast days are when the
      sadness and loneliness comes to call.

I go walking in the rain and no one knows the
      tears are making puddles except me.
No explanation or feelings need to be given
      for the emotion is covered you see.

I cannot even try to explain it to my own self
      so how can I expect another to see?
It seems like from the deep pain of my lost
      love I will never be free.

The whole country is under raindrops and
      it is something that is quite sad.
Are they sort of gloomy and down in spirit
      remembering what they once had?

Everyone's life goes on at its own speed
      and always simply in its own way.
But here I sit under this very dark and liquid
      sky and wishing for brighter day.

Elaine Long

GROWING OLD AND
LIFE'S SURPRISES

THE BODY QUICKLY FORGETS

I have never been this old before and that is a fact.
I guess that is why I don't know how my body will act.
The strength and endurance I once had is long gone.
It is weird how the loss makes me feel at risk and alone.

Balance and agility disappeared in the very same way.
On some days, a fall seems likely an ugly role to play.
My mind plays some dirty tricks too often now it seems.
I not only forget words, but often lose the whole scene.

It may seem funny to the reader, but it is so scary to me.
What if I forget faces long before I can no longer see?
My mirror has a mean intent and shows it when I gaze.
The image I see looking back leaves my mind in a haze.

It is depressing to feel and see one's body age and decline.
Body parts keep freezing and most especially my old mind.
Everything I start to do is either out of sight or out of reach.
My only option left is alerting others to old age, so I preach.

Life is like a rushing creek or perhaps some quick stream.
Each year takes away more abilities from me or so it seems.
You must go slowly but thoroughly all along your life's way.
Certainly and surely, minute-by-minute life is running away.

Do all you want to now while you can and put nothing off.
If you wait until later, your body at you will laugh and scoff.
The body just forgets how to be flexible, capable, and limber.
Muscles lose their knowhow or else they do not remember.

Old Age

Old age has too many unexpected surprises to say the very least.
No one ever mentioned that it also turns into a nasty, ugly beast.
They forgot to say the mind goes and in place the aches come.
About eye sight failure and wrinkles galore they remained mum.

Or the growing tendency one has of putting things off another day.
This seems to be quite a steadily increasing problem I have to say.
What about my get up and go cruelly disappearing without warning?
Though it could have been scared away by joint noise each morning.

Those golden years being so pretty is what I have always heard said.
But I also remember pretty golden leaves on trees soon end up dead.
I could once walk to the creek and then turnaround and run right back.
Now I sit and huff and puff and wheeze with the lungs all out of whack.

It is nearly becoming a half day chore in order to make myself a snack.
The other half is spent opening or closing the dang packaging sack.
No one told me gravity would turn evil and simply become a living hell.
Or that all body parts would droop and drop and flop and sag as well.

Once I stood straight and strong with lots of energy was almost fairly fit.
Now bent and tired and my purse is a drug store as well as first aid kit.
The short term memory has gone and I can't stop the brain cell seep.
It's safe to say my mind has passed the max and now has a big leak.

If I could remember where this poem was going, to finish it I would try.
Tidbits of long ago still clear, but long term memory is last to go by bye.
If an elderly person had enlightened me years ago about this old age.
I would have taken more time to smell the roses in my younger stage.

So take my heed all you folks, if most of your parts still work without pain.
Remember, you will not feel any younger than you are now; ever again.
As soon as one is born the clock starts ticking and they begin their trip.
Then youth will race to mid-life and on a banana peel into old age slip.

Elaine Long

I FELT OK UNTIL

I have decided that getting old will not be any picnic.
It takes too long to move around on my walking stick.
Any joint that happens to work hurts most of the time.
My brain won't cooperate with the right words I find.

Getting up sounds like a cereal, that contains a pop.
One knee or the other continues to cause me to hop.
The feet swell but yet the brain shrinks on most days.
Managing shoe laces and buttons require new ways.

Fingers freeze up and refuse to flex and forget to curl.
Nothing is like it once was here in this old age world.
I can't hear the dang TV until a commercial comes on.
My taste buds have bloomed out and now are all gone.

The newspaper print is smaller and not what it used to be.
I wonder why they are making it so difficult for me to see.
My arms grow shorter with each passing day so it seems.
There is not enough sleep to even allow a decent dream.

The doorsteps have grown steeper than they once were.
No one has ever asked me if that would be alright, no sir.
I have yet to understand how I can go to bed feeling good.
The next morning I would get my body up if only I could.

What battles did I fight in the night and lost most of them too?
When I was young even a half night sleep left me brand new.
This family of squatters named Ritis keeps on hanging around.
Of all these boys, it seems that old Arthur is the real clown.

It should be against the law for them to pester some old soul.
So it would suit me just fine if they were left out in the cold.
I seem to have felt ok until I was 39 for the twenty first time.
Since that day my body has refused to do right or to feel fine.

Take my warning, getting old is certainly not anything funny.
An old body can't be made young with any amount of money.
Do and have all the fun now while you are young and still able.
I did not know I would hurt more wearing the old woman label.

Elaine Long

THIS OLD AGE THING

The clutter has piled up and so did the dishes too.
There is sweeping to be done and bills are all due.
If I'm not behind on something; then I'm quite late.
All of the aspects of my life are now in a terrible state.

First retirement seemed to be all giggles and much fun.
It turned into an excuse not to get many things done.
Tomorrow is another day is not just funny but very true.
But the sad fact is tomorrow is something I never get to.

Then comes along this thing they called old menopause.
Pause is the operative word and is much of the cause.
It is the first part of getting old is what I have been told.
That wee bit of wisdom by its self is such a pain to behold.

What was once here is now there and badly out of shape.
I know this is true without using any old measuring tape.
Most of my joints sure don't work like they once could.
Sometimes now they act like they are made out of wood.

My mind flew away and went south a very long time ago.
But in actuality it didn't have a great distance in which to go.
My absent memory leaves a lot of room to wish and want.
Some days it works and then on some other days it just don't.

My get up must have gotten up and gone some other place.
Without it I sure can't expect to win much in this life's race.
Now if you find this information is cute and such funny stuff.
Or you think out there in the real world you have it quite tough.

You have work and schedules and deadlines and all those rules.
A battle is in the snarling traffic with all those idiots and fools.
Your best years are now while your mind and body work good.
My life would be much better too, if any work again I just could.

But my mind disappeared and to work once more I just can't.
All I can do is sit here and lose my glasses and rave and rant.
I must get up and get busy so I can get all my cleaning through.
Funny though I can't remember just what I had started to do.

OLD TIMERS KNEW BEST

Old timers would say, "Nothing ever stays the same."
I once thought it was just part of the old age game.
As I get older the truer their words have grown to be.
For instance how one was trained used to be the key.

In life and character the raising was how they would be.
Now days one goes haywire more often than not I see.
This generation of boys has something seriously wrong.
A part of their anatomy seems to be falling all day long.

Pants have pockets and strides down low at the knees.
All would be flashers if they bent over or had to sneeze.
An arm and hand is needed to hold everything together.
Do they think the style and the body grabbing are clever?

Some hold to their pants so down south they won't slide.
Or they would trip and fall or their back side couldn't hide.
Most of them seem to live only for their selves or for today.
Would they be helpful, or considerate to others, no way?

A respect for elders used to be almost a commandment.
Now most young people are hateful and authority resent.
No regard or any kind of integrity for their self or anyone.
Old timers had the right idea when all is said and done.

It is a good thing the old folks have finished their course.
To see youth actions of today they would talk till hoarse.
Far more changes than they could have ever envisioned.
Many young people of today are on a path for a collision.

If one was to say no would they be face to face with death?
As the gun smoke cleared there would not be anything left.
Yet this generation will lead the country in the future as well.
Will this be the day our country ends or takes a path to hell?

THE OLD GREY MARE

As the body grows old and years begin to show.
The mind gets weak and forgets all it should know.
Maybe it is vice versa but you get the general idea.
Whatever it is called gives one much worry to fear.

Years spent looking after others and their affairs.
Suddenly it seems many little things get in my hair.
Not to mention that my hair is on its way out too.
Plus my joints do not do what I want them to do.

Jobs once done in an hour now take a day or two.
After I finish I cannot remember if I got through.
My memory went out to lunch and then ran away.
I could even hide my own Easter eggs on any day.

There certainly is a lot of humor in this getting old.
It would be funnier if on someone else it were told.
If I hurry to do something, it is quite comical to face.
In a chase with peanut butter, I would lose the race.

Yet it appears the writing is not only on every wall.
It is also on the ceiling and scribbled down the hall.
This old grey mare simply is not what she used to be.
More importantly, youth again she won't be able to see.

No ability and strength to do the job or carry her weight.
For sooner than later, others for her will have to wait.
The final season of life is now slowly drawing to a close.
Old age on the mare rushed right in as everybody knows.

God knows when it will be time for a call from on high.
The good book reads there is an appointed time to die.
There is a good thing about this old age taking its toll.
Up in Heaven no one will ever again grow weak or old.

Elaine Long

YOU GOT TO BE KIDDING

You got to be kidding, if you are thinking I am sixty five.
Now my body parts just seem to be more like eighty five.
All my joints make embarrassing noises each time I arise.
Something has definitely gone very wrong with my eyes.

Each finger seems to have grown a devious mind of its own.
Some bend; or not, one freezes up, one makes me moan.
The knees surprise me without warning and just don't work.
They often send out a quick painful stab that makes me jerk.

The back and neck often connive on plans to lock up tight.
Big bags under my eyes make one think I've been in a fight.
My nose has long retired and only holds up my glasses now.
My old feet always seem to dictate daily activities somehow.

These old lungs went on disability in nineteen ninety seven.
Many times since then they have tried to send me to Heaven.
My taste buds have been in use so long they just up and died.
Some of my bones have this snapping disease I will confide.

I seem to have lost the remote to address a volume on my ears.
The only thing that does well is the switch that works the tears.
My aged mind I have saved for last for it's always out to lunch.
It is the thing I need and miss the most; and it is gone a bunch.

So I beg to differ when you say I will be sixty five and soon.
My body is just older than that so if you sing the birthday tune.
Sing clearly for all the miles on this body make me eighty five.
Of course at any age I can thank God's blessing for being alive.

GETTING OLD ISN'T ALL BAD

I am not worried for getting old isn't all bad from where I sit.
Some more freedom comes with aging and all that goes with it.
At times I'm forgetful but some things should be forgotten.
Then there are my ears that act like they are filled with cotton.

I have been blessed to live long enough to see some grey hair.
Many have died before their hair color caused them any care.
Broken hearts give strength, understanding and compassion.
The kind of things needed and never become old fashioned.

It is true my heart was broken over the loss of an adored mate.
Yet not living long enough to experience that love I would hate.
Laugh lines in the face prove life had something to smile about.
Not to have had things to laugh over would be so sad no doubt.

I am content and I like the kind of person I have become at last.
Easier to be positive but time to care what others think has passed.
I know I won't or do I want to live forever, but while I am still here.
My goal is to take one day at a time and live and love without fear.

Yes getting older means sometimes forgetful but that is alright.
But some parts of life are just as well forgotten and out of sight.
Wouldn't it be so nice to be selective about what things to forget?
All those sad or painful thoughts would not again on nerves sit.

There are few things or people in my life to make me happy anymore.
My fun will come from doing only the things which give me joy galore.
A rainbow of smiles in my heart and mind keep me from getting old.
If the body no longer works, I will still have those memories to unfold.

Elaine Long

AGE AND MILES AND SEASON

As I sit here in my usual place and ponder about the future.
Emotions of all kinds remind me my heart could use a suture.
It seems like age and miles and season are getting me down.
Little things normally ignored now hurt me more I have found.

This season of the year always seems to have a hold on me.
Yet on so many dark days a cloud of dread is all there is to see.
Could it be I am mentally against the milestone of getting so old?
Is it because I have so many good memories left for me to hold?

So much I need to get up and do yet I don't want to do any of it.
Part of it may be that I don't know where to start so here I just sit.
Tasks were once done without any hesitation or second thought.
They are now often completed by having the services all bought.

It may be from forgetting how, getting old, or not having an expert.
The loss of my confidence is chilling and is one more thing to hurt.
The fear is attempting to fix something and only creating a big jam.
I wonder sometimes it might be less stressful just to go on the lam.

The fact is of growing older than dirt plus having to face it all alone.
It is one of the harder tasks ahead from now on that I have known.
Maybe it is just depressing and sad to be soon turning sixty five.
I guess it is a blessing to have been around so long and be alive.

I know whatever it is that is getting me down is out of my control.
So, Lord I will put my faith and trust completely in you as I get old.
Only you know why I was chosen to walk this path and walk it alone.
Walk with me Lord in this season of life and bad feelings will be gone.

THIS FACT IS THE SAME

In all of one's life there is control in, of and over everything.
There is willpower to or not do this or that or to caution fling.
Knowledge is to know the difference between right and wrong.
The "mind over matter" rule over terrible things to stay strong.

Holding the tongue while an expert tells everything they know.
Exercising control when one would like to tell another where to go.
Having good manners and diplomacy and a great amount of tact.
Yet every fiber of one's being wants to reply, scream or fight back.

To smile and nod rather than frown over some disappointment.
Or stay calm and not scream when a love on to Heaven is sent.
One's entire life is rules and regulation and order to desires keep.
Control over desires and mostly to keep hurt feelings down deep.

From the cradle to the grave these things are constantly taught.
Doing the right things and restraining from what one ought.
Remaining silent when sharp replies would give some satisfaction.
Enduring the storms of life and attempting to control ones actions.

Life is a maze of restraints and rules and laws and so many don'ts.
Society mandates discipline over ones desires or needs or wants.
Yet all the years of learning and exhibiting all those kinds of control.
They all are totally removed and forgotten when one grows old.

Not any power to rule over one's final years left upon this earth.
This fact is the same no matter what is found to be one's worth.
It is sad that all of the confines of life fail one at the life's end.
All manners and ways and etiquette are all thrown to the wind.

Elaine Long

LESSONS LEARNED

UNTIL THEN

No matter what comes to stay on your shoulder.
Much worrying will quickly make you grow older.
It isn't over when some lady stands up and sings.
Nor is it even finished as the doctor's words ring.

One can walk each day alone with a heavy load.
They will stumble down the dark and rocky road.
One may feel lonely and left without a way to turn.
While waiting for the final results of a test to learn.

No one this side of God ever knows what lies ahead.
Nor will you know what will be your last words said.
Happiness and suffering on all of us will one day come.
How we accept it is what is important when all is done.

There is not any way I can feel the depth of your pain.
Nor do I have any power to make things right again.
Any sickness, pain, trouble or woe is each one's trial.
That lady or the doctor cannot predict your last mile.

God has put each one of us here and reason for good.
We will be here for only as long as He thinks we should.
Life can end tomorrow for any of us by God's own plan.
Until then I will live each day as my last as long as I can.

WONDER OF WONDERS

A mind cannot comprehend what a heart can take.
For it could not survive the ordeal of a heart break.
Sometimes all of life's troubles make us need a lifeline.
Much later, one will realize God was there all the time.

In one's life, there are problems and sometimes woes.
God is always close and completely directing the show.
When I do not have any idea of which way to turn or go.
He directs someone to touch a heart and let love flow.

God's love is magnificent and so kind and truly pure.
Over His children and creation He will forever endure.
The storms of life are very varied and always so many.
Those times answers evade, and of solutions, not any.

When a miserable heart has hurt so much it just aches.
It is at these times; it really cracks and then easily breaks.
Wonder of wonders have really to me come very true.
His unlimited mercy and plan constantly see me through

I often think of all the events which happened in my life.
My job was in all the years being a daughter, friend or wife.
Most of my family members have to Heaven now gone.
I have chosen not to be sad being left here nearly alone.

By counting my many blessings helped my heart to mend.
My appreciation is endless for both great family and friends.
I know love is just amazing and is truly wonderfully divine.
I thank you Lord, for always being to me so loving and kind.

Elaine Long

IT IS LIKE A BOOMERANG

Make an effort to throw your heart open wide every day.
By day's end, be sure you have given something away.
It could be in a warm smile to someone in some distress.
Or it might go in a call to a person whose life is in a mess.

Go to lunch with one who has dark grief that won't end.
For each of us have days we could certainly use a friend.
An unexpected phone call is as welcome as is good food.
A "thinking of you" card will always lift up a low mood.

Some coincidental meeting can be enhanced by a hug too.
One simply does not know what another is going through.
It is a good possibility that a hug is often missed the most.
Mostly dark lonely days and empty arms serve as the host.

All those doubts and fears build up like heavy weights to all.
Prayers offered in their name and God will sever grief's wall.
A "call me if you need me," does not always receive a reply.
But, a drop in without any purpose may dry tears in the eye.

A kind word or soft voice can do much for one's mental state.
Simply a pat on the back to confidence can a difference make.
An honest compliment can make one feel better and less blue.
All love that is given away is received again plus some anew.

To give something back to a person in the depths of great need.
No greater commandment than to praise God by a sincere deed.
A Good Samaritan it is time to be and spread it all over the land.
The Lord expects us to love one another and help when we can.

All of the emotions and deeds are not expensive items to share.
It does not require a monetary value to show we genuinely care.
Nor does it take too much time to share of one's heart and soul.
It is like a boomerang, not only returning, but it arrives tenfold.

FRIENDS AND FAMILY AND BEAUTY

When God designed and created everything that was ever to be.
No one but He was around for all the plans that you can now see.
Here thousands of years later, He still controls the perfect plan.
Though humans try, God does not allow it to be ruined by man.

The total minutes of every life is known to no one, except to Him.
The control of our destiny cannot be changed by anyone's whim.
The Bible says our days are numbered like the hair on our head.
His divine plan is what determines on which day we will be dead.

Without time to waste, therefore I have decided to live each day,
As either it is my last one or I will never again walk along this way.
If I live each day as a final one on earth, then all the love I will see.
Everything will be a lot clearer and I will enjoy all that is around me.

Friends, family and beauty are there to enjoy continually so much.
Completely seeing and feeling all things with an extra loving touch.
Then if today is not my last and yet another tomorrow I live to see.
How much more blest and helpful may the days of my life ever be.

I take much time to laugh with, live for and to others show love.
These are marvelous gifts God has graciously sent from above.
When my final day arrives and my last race has almost been run.
I will be at peace and ready to blissfully journey beyond the sun.

Elaine Long

ALONG THE JORDAN RIVER

Don't cry when my soul goes off to roam.
For I have only journeyed to my new home.
From where you are, I am not very far away.
You are one heartbeat away one sweet day.

Don't stand near me and grieve and weep.
I am not dead nor am I resting or asleep.
So look to God to wipe your tears all away.
I am safe with Him in my new home today.

Along the Jordan River for you I will wait.
There you and I will have a forever date.
Until then my love for you will never depart.
For now my spirit lives on within your heart.

Judge me only by the memory I leave behind.
Not by tangible or worldly things you may find.
Think of me when you look upon a happy face.
Recall all the good times we had in life's race.

Think of me often by some remembered word.
I hope "I love you" will be what you most heard.
Just know my memories of you are just as sweet.
Reminiscing for an eternity when again we meet.

NOTHING IS FOREVER

Someone I did not know, to another just recently said.
A thought I had known for years but have not ever read.
He said God would always allow the right people in your life.
By coming at the proper time or when you are facing some strife.

Some opportunities have a single purpose only once in a lifetime.
Those extra unusual events seem to have no reason or any rhyme.
God knows and sends the right one and always at the right time.
He sends them when our mountain is too rough or hard to climb.

It may be to lend a shoulder, or give strength, or an ability to lead.
God sends what we need to guide us in the way we should proceed.
It may be one with angelic attributes to help a heart to heal and mend.
It can be one with knowledge or know how to be more than a friend.

The gloom is thick and disappointment and fear of a future is unknown.
Someone is sent to fill the gap, or remove distress, until worry is all gone.
He will provide us with everything we require for each and every day.
All that is missing is we forget to ask for understanding when we pray.

The correct people will come at His command into a life for a reason.
It is God's decision if they are there for life or just stay for one season.
The right people are at the right time traveling across one's life path.
It is another of God's wonderful blessings allowing for love and laughs.

If someone moves in to stay, or passes through, or out of our life one day.
Their presence or leaving is or was not an accident but only God's way.
Nothing is forever and all of life's changes make one stronger grow.
In any trouble worry or woe, to face it alone, God will never let us go.

Elaine Long

HAVE A GOING AWAY PARTY

They were born in the same hospital in nineteen forty five.
From the day they were wed love began to grow and thrive.
She was there for all the good or bad with the love of her life.
Nothing could ever be more important than being his wife.

She would adore and miss him greatly until her dying day.
Wishing again to hear his voice and what he had to say.
The only thing to help her survive was hugging his memory.
Even memories held on to do not ever hug back you see.

The rest of her life was trying to decide on which way to start.
The cold winds of sorrow always blew over her broken heart.
She never again was completely living after they had to part.
It was plain for all to see that when he left he took her heart.

When the final day on this earth has arrived for her at last.
Instead of grieving or being sad, let her go home with class.
Throw her a going away party and have a grand celebration.
The day she has waited for has arrived with so much elation.

Make the heaven bound event the grandest celebration of all.
A great state of mind she was in when her angel came to call.
Celebrate, not grieve for the happy couple are together again.
They will have very much to catch up on since way back then.

All that time she was alone, but he always stayed on her mind.
Time spent reliving some memories that were of the best kind.
Finally once again they are together and walking side by side.
When she dies will be her happiest day since her love died.

It will be a joyous time in Heaven for those two have again met.
The stars that night will be the brightest ones to ever shine yet.
So celebrate with them with a going away party here below.
Knowing you too are Heaven bound and just waiting to go.

TREASURES OF THE HEART

When one has lived with another for more than thirty years
This lifetime of memories and moments are held so dear.
As long as the mind remembers, the past remains alive.
All of the present and future wrapped in love will thrive.

Remembrances are shared just like a joint bank account.
Warm recollections are deposited and continue to mount.
All of the past is a part of the present as long as both live.
After a death, all of the mental recalls have much to give.

Some of the thoughts and reminders will avert the fears.
Yet no matter how sweet the memory, it will produce tears.
Every life is all about memories in one way or in another.
Each one influences the life of all the sisters and brothers.

People, places or things have made us what we are today.
Even after a death, these important helps do not go away.
Memories are much more special after a devastating loss.
Keeping the nostalgia close is important whatever the cost.

Some reflections are sweet and yet some others are sour.
Actually one's frame of mind can change within the hour.
Recalling the good times do become treasures of the heart.
In a life some precious thoughts will forever remain a part.

Happy musings turn pain into strength and scars into pearls.
Reflecting and remembering are company in a lonely world.
Memories and time do much toward healing a broken heart.
Completing this hurdle is a step toward making a new start.

The memory of the just
Is blessed
Proverbs 10:17

Elaine Long

PANIC

I am standing all alone in the big empty place.
I am so glad right now, I have no one to face.
My insides are churning with a lump and a knot.
An anxiety attack seems to be the problem I got.

I guess how to keep breathing I must have forgot.
Other times productive breaths I simply have not.
I cannot imagine what happened to bring this on.
But, if I cannot breathe, I will soon die here alone.

I sure could rest easier if this panic was all gone.
Though in my mind the anxiety has now grown.
I cannot get it to cease with fan for air or chill.
Just call it panic or anxiety, or whatever one will.

I simply now have no choice except to take a pill.
It is not of the mind, for smothering is very real.
Now what can I do until that old pill takes effect?
My only choice for now is pant for air and sweat.

I must concentrate now on out thinking the pain.
Stabbing throbs in my neck go on and on again.
If no relief comes soon, then it might just explode.
Nerves are going crazy and creating a heavy load.

I wish I knew what caused such panic to unfurl.
I know it got full attention here in my little world.
It is not so bad, so some smart aleck would say.
They just have not had to fight to breathe any way.

I sure am hoping it will soon pass away from me.
However, for now it definitely will not set me free.
I may never know what has brought this panic on.
Yet without some relief soon, I can't even phone.

Forcing myself to think and then to write it down.
I must in case I cannot talk whenever I am found.
Maybe these words will at least leave them a clue.
It seems to help take my mind off my worry too.

THE PRESSURE RISES

Over the many years the different things on my mind wore.
Some type situations and emotions have been there galore.
Today for the most part all of my life is very quiet and plain.
That is very important to me and it helps to keep me sane.

I control all of the noise level that comes within my space.
I do turn the TV off and I don't hear about the human race.
Picking some less busy times to go shopping is what I do.
Then I don't have to hear the brat's noise I am not use to.

When I have reached my limits of racket I have got to go.
Don't ask or be so concerned or all the whys want to know.
You can't know how noise affects me, its ok I understand.
If I don't know why myself, I can't expect anyone else can.

I hear incessant noises or music and then some loud chatter.
It frankly makes me nervous and at wits end with all the clatter.
For whatever reason it reaches a point I just want to scream.
The anxiety grows and the awareness is like one bad dream.

Most of the panic is on me and others near will not ever know.
The pressure rises and if I don't move quickly, it will overflow.
Sometimes it's others talking without taking a breath or a break.
To keep my last bit of pride or dignity, a fast exit I have to take.

I once thought all my nerves were worn out and or long gone.
But I have decided that one or two of them are still hanging on.
They seem to grow more frayed and all stressed out each day.
Until at last nerves just snap and then my feet are on their way.

A nerve pill might help me but what about all the noise makers?
If I can't escape the sound someone might need an undertaker.
I don't know why noisy people or places can get me all uptight.
Or why it just gets louder until I want to run away into the night.

Whatever the reason or excuse loud noise makes me act crazy.
Everyone will have more fun if I stay home and simply play lazy.
My sweet dog likes peace and quiet too so we get along just fine.
So talk on, laugh and be loud and I won't lose my poor old mind.

Elaine Long

IN SPITE OF IT

It is usually not very hard to tell what one is thinking.
But it is almost impossible to know how one is feeling.
The calm mind all by itself can think all things through.
But it adds worries, stress and those sad feelings too.

It takes very many words to describe the turmoil inside.
Panic, anxiety, or the trouble one is trying hard to hide.
A heavy cloud still hangs so low over most of every day.
There is hesitation to show much weakness in any way.

Events in life, the genes and yes nerves all play a part.
To determine one's strength or failure right from the start.
The ever increasing loss of interest also disheartens a soul.
Adding a daily dose of melancholy helps one to grow old.

The weakness and fatigue and tiredness are all I can feel.
Content to gaze out in space and no desire to move is real.
Sometimes help may come in the form of an old nerve pill.
Most of the time it works and over emotions it cast a chill.

There are times aggravations will keep it from working well.
On those days life simply seems to come straight from hell.
All are deep feelings that totally encase this old aching heart.
They are days filled with pain and loneliness from the start.

Maybe the outward appearance is ok but inside it is a mess.
But those feelings will stop one day when life ends I guess.
How one handles all of life's burdens isn't always the concern.
It is what one becomes in spite of it by what one has learned.

THINGS I WOULD CHANGE IF I COULD

Many things need so much changing in this world today.
The scores of items cannot leave enough words to say.
I would not change any personal status or any residence.
Much more important things would take the precedence.

Only the top five things upon my list to modify I will tell.
If that small number was changed life would then be swell.
First I would change this country back to a much safer way.
The problems with crime and the economy would go away.

Next I would stop the nation's animosity against one another.
All countries would treat each other like a sister and a brother.
Never again would war or conflict take lives of our very young.
Only peace would be enjoyed and the goodwill spread with fun.

The third thing would be turn back the clock 30 or more years.
Really far enough back to be long before all the cares and tears.
Yet all of today's knowledge and the friends would still remain.
A great ability to love with shoulders to lean on through all pain.

Another change I would make would be a maximum noise limit too.
Volume could not be turned up loud no matter what one would do.
Finally the fifth thing to change would be something so very small.
I'd remove all pain and any hurt feelings forever from one and all.

It is wishful thinking to want to change these things I know I cannot.
I do believe changing these items would help the whole world a lot.
All I can do is pray for God to change all in the world that is wrong.
Then the world will be a much better place where all could get along.

Elaine Long

IF FOR ONLY AN INSTANT

For just a little while imagine the worst feeling in all your life.
Or possibly the biggest sense of loss that caused you strife?
Think of being lost somewhere with no one or thing in sight.
Though wishing to see a familiar face with all of one's might.

Depict being left alone in a strange place with no one to call.
Capture an image of running in darkness on an endless hall.
Try to picture a child peering longingly inside of a candy store.
For whatever reason they can't have what is beyond the door.

Remember awaking from a bad dream and shaking with fright?
Sleep then out of the question for terror remained for the night.
One can feel this desperation from within and feel the weight.
You may not without having personal knowledge contemplate.

If for only an instant you can touch this numbness or emotion.
Then you could get a glimpse, hint or maybe have some notion.
In our society the trend is to always be in twos or a coupled pair.
If you are without a partner, then you have no right being there.

How devastating it really is to live in this world alone as a widow.
Don't assume I am exaggerating, or that I am simply being bitter.
The panic and anxiety prevent one from thinking correct or straight.
It's in knowing one can't breathe unless and until the pain abates.

I know too you cannot have any idea of how this position really feels.
My hope is and will be that in all the days of your life, you never will.
So don't think too hard of me when your invitation I tactfully decline.
I'll just stay home and not have to pretend I am ok, if you don't mind.

BE KIND

Someone you know may have a heavy burden of the heart.
A sick spouse or the role of caregiver is a very hard part.
Another problem or some need arises around every turn.
Everyday has more to do and another side effect to learn.
Not just physical toil and labor to tire one completely out.
But with all of the emotional demands create so much doubt.

You may see the stress in their face and want to speak and say.
"I see the problem and my idea for you will be a better way."
All the components of a fix you may have in your great plan.
The answers to the problems are simple and you know you can.
Well friend, let me inject into your plan, just one small thought.
Right before on the recipes and solutions your tongue gets caught.

A caregiver has another reason you can't have in your solving mix.
They hold the key to it and no one else can the problem ever fix.
See the giver of care also has it entwined into their loving heart.
They also had that special ingredient of love from the very start.
If you haven't walked in their shoes then you just cannot know.
The load gets heavier by the day yet there is only one way to go.

Going forward hour by hour no matter how much there is to do.
Tending to the needs of that adored one is more than physical too.
All the love and protection yet fear of what is somewhere ahead.
Knowing this is the only way to live until the loved one is dead.
The truth of the situation is the giver of care will give their very all.
Whatever it takes and for how long they will meet the need and call.

Elaine Long

They cannot listen to you; or what you want; or do it any other way.
Their heart will only allow them to do all the care giving every day.
For if they should listen and leave for a little while to get some rest.
Their heart and mind would remain and just cause them more stress.
Be kind and only prayers and support to the caregiver freely give.
After this role ends, only with themselves they will also have to live.

The only thing to ask them do now is their energy to try and pace.
So there will be enough strength for all emotions they have to face.
By the side of the precious one is the only place they want to be.
You can always help them the most from upon your bended knee.
Ask God to give them physical and mental strength just enough.
Strong faith and hope for the journey when life really gets tough.

IT GETS ONE'S FULL ATTENTION

All of the walls of anxiety are now steadily closing in.
This inability to get enough oxygen is lurking again.
A frightening sense of fear and unease is all around.
Any positive thought of action just cannot be found.

Panic and the terror inside are definitely on the rise.
I get into the middle of trouble almost before I realize.
Desperately gasping for air does not bring any relief.
I hope the brain will function despite the oxygen thief.

This is a thumbnail view of distress as anxiety attacks.
Describing it completely is impossible and that is a fact.
Not knowing what causes it and why it quickly appears.
Wondering if I will live past it is one of the worst fears.

For I never know just what to do when facing it all alone.
Without getting any relief quickly my life will soon be gone.
The horrible feeling of an attack may have come from hell.
When the sensation starts it really sets up a warning bell.

I have never felt more helpless than when held in its clutch.
For every fiber of my being is affected by its rough touch.
All of my full attention is given to the fear of a panic attack.
It's like walking around with a heavy weight across my back.

I wonder if an anxiety strike will appear suddenly at night.
Quietly sleeping safely through it would certainly be alright.
Though I doubt it would be possible to miss all of this horror.
Or not to have all those bad memories of it come tomorrow.

Under the watchful eye of God hopefully this I will live past.
By morning light it will have ended and be over for me at last.
I'm ok until the next time without any warning it's back again.
Yet as long as I keep surviving it, I guess it won't do me in.

TAKE NOTHING FOR GRANTED

We have always assumed the sun would rise tomorrow.
We expect it to be someone else to have all the sorrow.
Everything, we simply know is going to turn out all right.
Then that sun will set like it always has just before night.

We take too much for granted in the course of every day.
We think of any trouble happening to us and say, "no way".
We tend to believe we have lots of time left in which to live.
Therefore also have plenty of years yet to love and to give.

What we depend on greatly may only be here for just today.
Some of those precious things may never again pass our way.
In the blink of an eye; one's life can be changed forevermore.
Destruction or sickness or pain can rain down in a downpour.

Never assume tomorrow will come or that life will be the same.
Treat each day as if it will be the last one played in life's game.
Say each goodbye like it had to last until we see Heaven's gate.
For one can never presume if either party will survive their fate.

So tell them how much you love them and hug them very tight.
That death angel often takes our loved ones deep in the night.
Tomorrow may not come for you, or be in God's plan to send.
Never depend on there being another time for hearts to mend.

Do not leave anything unsaid, as love crosses your mind say it.
Share with others as your hearts bond together and as love is lit.
Take nothing for granted for the length of our journey is unknown.
Now is the time to express feelings or the moment may be gone.

Live every day of life just as though it was going to be your very last.
Love as if the loss of some loved ones was in an immediate forecast.
Pray as though the Lord was coming back tomorrow for each of us.
Another chance may not be granted and each moment is so precious.

WE GET THROUGH

Sometimes one's life takes a detour down a long hard road.
Mile after lonely mile we withstand with a heart heavy load.
God is there simply waiting to push, pull or carry us along.
Yet human nature causes us to try and accomplish it alone.

A rough excursion and the rewards are rare and far between.
Only those who cared for a loved one can know what I mean.
There is not any glory in to be entrusted with a caregiver role.
It is the best thing known for making one quickly feel very old.

So many disappointments and setbacks always clutter the way.
Sheer stress and exhaustion greet one at the end of every day.
One does not know their strength before taking this occupation.
They also discover things that can cause the most aggravation.

Not any other tiredness seems to be felt nearly so sharp or deep.
Even with fatigue in the bones, it is still very hard to find sleep.
There are too many roles to play and too many shoes to try to fill.
After a while, the days and the surprises cease to seem to be real.

The solutions to the roadblocks were not ever found in any book.
We can get through situations but cannot promise how we will look.
Though the footsteps mostly were unsteady, we don't regret a mile.
Some tears often desired yet kept well hidden beneath one's smile.

That which does not kill us, is in fact supposed to make us stronger.
At the time it seems one cannot hold on or out for very much longer.
One foot in front of the other will finally find the lonely road's end.
Hopefully then with God's help can one's body and heart ever mend.

Elaine Long

LOVE REMAINS THERE

They had so many wonderful years of sweet love and trust.
Maybe had a misunderstanding or two but very little fuss.
Loving and giving and always being each other's friend.
An assurance was of kindness each for the other to depend.

As the time flew by, their hearts entwined closer every year.
There is something about soul mates that will forever be dear.
They knew their union was sweetly created in Heaven above.
It will forevermore be overflowing with a special kind of love.

These words were so simple to think of and then write down.
For it is not hard at all to write about one's paradise found.
The easiest words always come from deep within the heart.
Love remains there even after death of one split them apart.

That special love has been lived and in each one's heart felt.
A true and a unique gift always made each other's heart melt.
On a great miracle of sweet love and trust, we always did agree.
I am eternally thankful for our life of love that God gave to me.

The Mark on Your Heart

If a kind person leaves a mark on your heart.
The indention of the print will always be there.
All the memories of it from you will never part.
It can be from a friendly touch or deed or care.

It might have come from suffering of a great loss.
If from having fallen out of an emotion called love.
Whatever trouble or love your heart has to cross.
The pains of your world God will see from above.

The love and concern is of your very good friend.
It makes the darkest day suddenly turn so bright.
This will stay in and on your mind until the end.
The mark this friend leaves is never out of sight.

It also can come from a love that is so very dear.
It captures your feelings and of course your heart.
It takes your breath away and the love is very clear.
This is the print that will make the deepest mark.

God always knew what He was doing from the start.
We forget He designed us so feelings we can hide.
God put the heart there for all these loves to mark.
He knew we would need extra warm feelings inside.

Elaine Long

ONE PERSON'S TREASURE

The main goal people have from the time one is grown.
It is to acquire some things of value for their very own.
Like keeping up with the Joneses or just getting ahead.
The aim for neat possessions is there until one is dead.

This concept continues as the objects mount up untold.
Years roll by and finally the American dream grows old.
But the children of the collector do not value all this stuff.
Else room for their toys and the elder's too is not enough.

One person's treasure is merely just another one's trash.
It holds no sentimental value, only plans to sell it for cash.
It is sad the kids now only think of things with dollar signs.
Some say they care but it is easy to read between the lines.

Each one's estate turns out to be about the same one day.
A person's belongings usually serve to get in another's way.
Maybe the "save it mode" comes from growing up with less.
That would explain how one ends up with such a big mess.

Another idea would be for the owner to have a great big sale.
Selling it off and only leaving a humorous yarn for them to tell.
With the sale money, take a trip and spend all the inheritance.
A value of one's possessions would then not be left to chance.

Today the throw away world is just the young ones latest style.
All seem to have the donation center number on the speed dial.
The future adults will not ever have a problem with accumulation.
For now they throw things away without any kind of hesitation.

It is depressing that children don't share their parent's interest.
At times the young generation put some elder's nerves to a test.
It seems one has to get old before of family things they grow fond.
It might be nice to make a kid sensitive by waving a magic wand.

THEY TAKE IT WITH THEM

All my life I heard that when it becomes time for one to go.
They don't take anything home with them, least of all woe.
Many years I naturally assumed it was a fact and was true.
For no one needs anything when they rise beyond the blue.

Dad always said no pockets will be found in the shrouds.
When one goes home to heaven, there beyond the clouds.
Until I felt grief's dreadful pain I assumed this had to be true.
But now I am of the conviction, that some correction is due.

When a loved one dies, they take with them so many things.
A great amount leaves this earth with them on angel wings.
They first take whatever caused the sunshine's brightest rays.
Without them near; everyday turns into continual sad rainy days.

The once beautiful moon has left like the twinkling stars at night.
Gone is the magical glow of the Christmas tree with sparkling lights.
All the Christmas spirit and wonder of the season disappeared too.
Now Christmas like every other day is just one more to go through.

The beauty of spring or joy or lazy days of summer are no more.
All of those things suddenly missing are just too much to ignore.
The happiness and meaning that anything held was taken from me.
It must have gone with him too for it is no longer here for me to see.

I had been wrong or misinformed for it all left when he went away.
Along with everything that had any importance to me up to that day.
So no longer do I believe one goes empty handed when they die.
Many things were lost forever when my loved one went to the sky.

Death is a thief of love and life and in all of the psychological aspects.
There is always some reason and so to Heaven I mean no disrespect.
 I am glad for at least I know what happened to my treasured things.
They're in good hands and one day again with their keeper I will sing.

Elaine Long

SAY WHAT IS ON THE HEART NOW

We have already traveled so far down this life's road.
At times it was and is an unexpected and heavy load.
Sometimes there was not any time for saying goodbye.
The ones left behind grieving could only weep and cry.

Let's not let this sad thing ever happen to us anymore.
Always say what's on the heart before going out the door.
Tell them how much lasting love you have for them too.
Lovingly relating just how much their lives mean to you.

Then let's make a pact that will last forevermore to us all.
Whenever life's unexpected action on one of us must fall.
Do not let wishes or any guilt ever be left or sneak inside.
To haunt the heart remaining here after a love has died.

Never put off until tomorrow what words can be said today.
The more someone says, "I love you", the easier it is to say.
Love expressed grows even lovelier as the time goes on.
The memory becomes sweeter with the departed one gone.

Until then and before the sun sets; freely your love express.
Don't leave it unsaid for the loved one to wonder or guess.
Instead of sadness we will be contemplating again to meet.
Together in heaven all loved ones to joyfully, lovingly greet.

There our life will not have pain or sorrow or never end.
For eternity we can be with loved ones family and friend.
Then we will stay forever with wonder and complete awe.
As we see more beauty and love than anyone ever saw.

THE FINAL CHAPTER

Dad's mood was low and his job ahead was sad and grim.
It was time to move on but wanting to include each of them.
There was a need to close this final chapter of her sweet life.
Four sons had lost their mother and he had lost his dear wife.

He had a need and desire to include them once and for all.
In choosing keepsakes and mementos each received a call.
One son was close by and came; but two others too far away.
The youngest needing more love and support had little to say.

But he finally agreed to come on home and be with his Dad.
For that they will forever be thankful and happy and glad.
Each one needed the other to work through many a sad task.
In doing so, each one created a memory that will last and last.

The bonding together again and their love was so evident.
The light hearted expressions and fun seemed heaven sent.
Neither one will ever know how much to the other it meant.
But each one acted at ease and at peace and so content.

The sad duty of closing one's estate is never an easy one.
But it was made so much softer with the help of two sons.
Maybe they grew closer and loved each other a little more.
As they finished this phase of life and closed one more door.

How fast the days flew and soon the short time had passed.
Sadly each one of them knew this mood could not forever last.
Yet the feelings were changed and mellowed and for the best.
Now maybe Dad and the sons have finally found some rest.

They had come together to ease some heart ache and pain.
Hopefully made each realize they can once more live again.
That life must go on for the ones who have been left behind.
It is easier if each one lets their emotions and hearts entwine.

Elaine Long

PARADISE IS
AT THE BEACH

THE ISLAND

Oh how wonderful coming back to this island is for me.
All surrounded by water almost as far as the eye can see.
Back to another world and far from the clutches of reality.
Casting worries to the wind allowing the mind to run free.

The past is gone, future unclear and the present at hand.
It allows the atmosphere to sift over one's body like sand.
Beach time is serene with comforting feeling and so daring.
The sun, waves and cloudless sky are each gently sharing.

The solitude of the atmosphere really soothes one's soul.
While gazing in reverence as yet another miracle unfolds.
No rude intrusion of worries or any loneliness or deep fears.
The inner peaceful feeling as though cleansed by ones tears.

It leaves for a short time and troubles of life fall far behind.
Here in this place between earth and heaven that is divine.
Harmony with loved ones made more priceless in the view.
The seclusion of one's mood and mind are lessened too.

While the beach and waves glitter under the stars at night.
It takes on new dimensions when accented by the moonlight.
This beauty is of the earth and sky and surf and white sand.
It is only a small glimpse of the great power of God's hand.

A rhythm of the waves flows over the spirit and in the mind.
It is in a peace and tranquility so difficult at times to find.
Most of life's role is to give, yet on the island one can take.
Till one's cup runs over with love with each new day break.

THE SUNRISE

All of the eastern sky is ablaze with brilliant glory.
Magnificent colors across the clouds tell the story.
An artist could not begin to capture the great scene.
Words cannot start to describe this beautiful thing.

A camera only endeavors to record the smallest part.
By viewing it in person one can store it in their heart.
The sunrise is only the beginning of a fresh new day.
What one does with it makes it ok or end in dismay.

Witnessing a sunrise from the beach is the best place.
So spectacular it has to be like a bit of heaven's taste.
Colors like a rainbow together in a magnificent blend.
Though it takes the breath away, it is too pretty to end.

As if on cue, the birds hush and the wind stands still.
Peace is with quiet and calmness and yet with it a chill.
The horizon begins to glow and the sun comes in view.
A sight so utterly astounding it allows the soul to renew.

The sun wakes up the earth and all within it each day.
It is such an astounding majesty and in an amazing way.
Such perfect splendor could have only come from above.
It is one more way for all to see a visual of God's love.

Thank you my Lord for such an array of lovely colors to see.
It sends nice thoughts of just how beautiful heaven must be.
I can only marvel at the awesome sight of each new day.
Lord your paintbrush has the master's touch in every way.

Elaine Long

Sunrise at the Beach

It is the continuous waves billowing at the shore.
Along the horizon the dark sky changes some more.
The subtle light in the Eastern sky begins to show.
Dawning of a new day with splendor begins to glow.

Colors are of every hue reflecting against a velvet sky.
The brilliance and beauty of God's sunrise is nigh.
They bounce back on the shimmering water of the gulf.
Describing the beauty of the scene words aren't enough.

The sun rising slowly like a beacon of Heaven's light.
That can only be described as a truly breathtaking sight.
It lights up sea foam and sky and puffy clouds above.
A mixture of loveliness is suspended only by God's love.

The viewing of a glorious event stirs on deep in the soul.
Peace and contentment deep inside while the eyes behold.
This lovely scene could only come from the Master's hand.
It is a masterpiece untouchable by any artist known to man.

So marvelous it must pale in comparison to Heaven's view.
God has all colors in the rainbow to make each day brand new.
As the sun majestically arises and shines from its resting place,
It lends a glimpse of God's perfect creation and of His grace.

SUNSET

The sun descends slowly to the bottom of a western sky.
It had warmed the earth with sun light from way up high.
I watched with awe and wonder as the sun said good bye.
The lovely day slowly ended and I tried hard not to cry.

A flaming glow commands my attention at the close of day.
The magnificent scene is simply incredible in every way.
A red sky is blazing amid the sun's final show and last glow.
Night will soon be closing in with a final curtain on the show.

It is like a spectacular ball from Heaven coming down fast.
Soon the show will be over and the sun will settle at last.
All color drains from the sky and then the twilight appears.
The end of another day is here and I can give God my fears.

The evening shadows remind me the day is almost gone.
What have I done with the time since I watched the dawn?
The time slipped away so quickly and I do not know where.
The sun and salt air with waves and sand are one big blur.

I should have accomplished something during this fine day.
I will do better if God allows me a tomorrow to walk this way.
He surely understands for He put the beauty here to behold.
On His creation I could gaze for years for it would not get old.

Such calmness is in the ending of what had been a good day.
I watched in peaceful reflection as God put the sun away.
Thank you Lord for so much beauty you lovingly send to us.
All the joy and bliss that fills our souls in your love we trust.

As Close to Paradise

An endless attraction has pulled us back once again.
This is a mixture of waves and views and all the sand.
The lure to return to this place has a foothold on us all.
It is basically all about the sights and sounds sweet call.

As we watch a sunrise over the rolling water of the gulf.
The words cannot be found to describe it well enough.
The magnificent beauty simply unfolds before one's eyes.
It takes one's breath away just watching God's sunrise.

One thousand pictures cannot begin to capture the view.
Only the eye can give full measure to colors of every hue.
Dear God, for the blessing of such beauty, we thank you.
Lord, forgive the ones who do not praise you for it too.

Humanity could never compete with the Master's hand.
We see breath catching beauty all over this glorious land.
The shore is as close to paradise as one here can ever be.
It must pale in comparison to Heaven yet ahead to see.

ONLY AT DAWN

The splendor of dawn is really something beautiful to see.
The proper words to describe it are not possible from me.
Such radiance is to marvel at when dawn lights the shore.
Each new color has more warmth in it than a minute before.

The water sparkles like diamonds in a background of blue.
Some velvet clouds in front of the huge sky burst into view.
The total array of fascination nearly takes ones breath away.
A bright single sunbeam silently begins casting a bright ray.

It continues to rise higher in the horizon until it lights the day.
Long awaited for but suddenly is here and quickly lights a way.
Slowly the sunrise spreads its beautiful colors on a waiting sky.
This awesome sight cannot ever be fully grasped by human eye.

The sand constantly changing colors as the sun begins to glow.
Often at sunrise a soft breeze starts and gently begins to blow.
The sun slowly appears over the horizon from its hiding place.
Only at this time can one look briefly into the sun's bright face.

A multitude of cameras could not this scene completely capture.
Somehow I think it may be but a tiny preview of the future rapture.
The way the sky and gulf and dawn come together at break of day.
On the beach to witness it makes one feel close to God I must say.

A glowing morning has arrived from across the gulf for all to see.
Such a breathtaking sight God sends to us each day and for free.
A masterpiece splendid it could have only come from God's hand.
Such perfection makes one almost hear music of an angel's band.

Elaine Long

A MASTERPIECE

When the time comes and the sun wakes up the earth.
The scene is more priceless than any money is worth.
All of the colors known come together by God's hand.
A masterpiece appears from the master all over the land.

It is expertly framed by the sky and sand and lovely gulf.
Day after day taking numerous pictures is never enough.
Some pictures can be worth more than a thousand words.
God's sunrise can't be expressed even in a million words.

The beauty of God's creation is overlooked so many times.
Maybe it isn't noticed because too much is on one's mind.
If so it denies one of the calming effects of such loveliness.
Such majestic beauty is too good to sleep through and miss.

From sunrise the sun moves toward heaven at a fast pace.
The many colors fade as the bright sun rises to take its place.
Dancing and sparkling over the surface of the waves in the sea.
It adds dimension to the white caps on the water for all to see.

Though the sun will continue on and can make the day so hot.
I had rather see the sunrise each morning when it is only a dot.
The master will forever be in control of this wondrous creation.
I openly thank God for the splendor of sunrises over this nation.

LET ME COUNT THE WAVES

My favorite pastime is counting all of the waves I can see.
It may be idle laziness but it is complete relaxation for me.
Others may not understand what makes this task so right.
The wave sounds relieve my stress and allow rest at night.

Each time a force of water meets the shore and the sand.
A comfort of peace warms my soul like a soft loving hand.
Let me count the waves and tell everyone all it does to me.
The calming effect of the beach is splendid to feel and see.

The dolphins and birds add wonderful scenes to behold.
Sitting for hours taking in the sights does not ever get old.
The warmth and brightness of the sun enhances the view.
The rays on the water create colors of every known hue.

The surf can thunder with all of its fury and force so great.
Like a massage, it chases pain away and my worries wait.
The frothy white caps stand up and out in distinctive detail.
Sometimes the wind blows softly or similar to a small gale.

Those soothing sounds shake the cobwebs from my mind.
No other place I have seen compares to peace here I find.
The sky with white wispy clouds blends in a water of blue.
Simply being at the beach cleanses mind and body anew.

Joy is an early morning on the beach in the quiet of sunrise.
Surrounded by splendid beauty is a miracle before my eyes.
Nowhere else is God's presence felt so loving or so strong.
This fine scene must be similar to having Heaven on loan.

A GIFT FROM THE WAVES

It is as unblemished and as near perfect as a cloudless sky.
The varied collection is of scenes which cause one to sigh.
Good intentions are so many when traveling to the beach.
When the time was over pure serenity had been reached.

A tired body and troubled mind take the first priority.
Creating rest and relaxation and letting the soul go free.
While the tide removes pain and ache from the heart.
Many of the thoughts are gently caressed from the start.

Finally, the mind recharges and comes to life once again.
All the time spent at the beach is great with sweet friends.
The lazy waves smooth the white sand and a troubled mind.
Discovering a more relaxing place would be hard to find.

The salt air and the sound of the waves soothe the soul.
The depth of calmness and peace can't be described or told.
Not even one cloud beneath a sapphire blue and bright sky.
Below, on the sand the tumbling frothy surf catches the eye.

The daring, brave seagulls are diving and always in search.
They swoop down quickly as if from some unknown perch.
A sandy and sunny beach bordered by dunes of white sand.
It gives an aura of tranquility never to be duplicated by man.

The breezy waves emitting a soft sea spray across the wind.
It simply makes one feel clean from within as aches rescind.
More of the seaweed and shells come to shore with each tide.
A travel yarn each one could tell but will not show or confide.

The scenes will cause one to want to just stand or sit and stare.
Even for just a little while, the view removes most every care.
Nowhere else on earth could any more relaxing scenery ever be.
It is peaceful to walk on the sand along the shore by the sea.

THE BUBBLING FOAM

One simply cannot live forever alone on an island and hide.
So they must keep some part of that place with them inside.
Never losing the tranquility and quiet one always finds there.
The relaxed mood felt inside could be caused by that salt air.

For a few minutes every day return to the island in the mind.
It allows enough peace and solitude for one to be able to find.
They can cast out worries and fears and leave them behind.
Allowing a spirit of calmness sometimes found in good wine.

It is the beach, or seaside, or coast, or the gulf or the shore.
No matter what it is called it is a paradise and so much more.
The time spent at water's edge is serenity in a relaxing calm.
While the birds dive; the wind just rustles in the trees of palm.

The tide is constantly tugging at the sand all along the beach.
With the waves breaking and capping just barely out of reach.
The pleasant sounds are of the water slapping along the sand.
It bathes the soul with a peaceful bliss like nothing else can.

The bubbling foam peaks as all of the waves crash and run.
Each new wave seems to crest over the back of the last one.
God in His infinite wisdom planned everything His own way.
Miracles and marvels of His design greet us on each new day.

Elaine Long

THE SONG OF THE WAVES

The gulf today is like a body of both gravity and motion.
It churns around with an inner turmoil of sharp emotions.
The waves are influenced by the unseen swift undertow.
Pulling and tugging from underneath like feelings I know.

The underlying current has a quick effect on everything.
Sometimes a big wave seems to suddenly take on wings.
It is a time nicely refreshed and renewed by the beach view.
Then the tide comes back in and the motions began anew.

Sand dunes are held together by big bunches of sea oats.
Where nearby the surf often appears to foam and then float.
The roar of the crashing waves is often like an angry blast.
Quickly turns into sheets of glass as the waves rest at last.

It becomes clear water lapping peacefully along the shore.
The angry surf like pain is often for a little while, no more.
The soft and gentle song of the waves has now been sung.
Sitting by the gulf with sounds and sights is so much fun.

It allows a wonderful view and a sense of calmness inside.
A restful feeling and relaxation so rarely felt on the outside.
The problems of the world seem far away while at the beach.
It is like being in a safe and warm cocoon and out of reach.

Empty Shells at the Shore

The many varied shells are lying scattered all along the shore.
They are not holding on to any life as they did once before.
All the lovely shells were shattered by the force of the waves.
As God's infinite plan comes full circle in the way life plays.

The shells have lost their purpose and now are cast away.
It serves as a gentle reminder of feelings of many a day.
The waves come so lively, yet rapidly all die upon the sand.
They will not be of any more value, or have use for again.

Even footprints in the sand all fade and quickly disappear.
Not like the endless worry or sometimes the intense fear.
The beach is grand yet can at times also be somewhat sad.
One can walk there alone and recall times of good and bad.

Two people are like shell halves coming together to make one.
Joined at the heart so long then broken apart and undone.
All resent change though it is only a step in the process of life.
Nevertheless, change cuts through the heart like a sharp knife.

Returning to the edge of the shore one reminisces all over anew.
The broken shells much like a broken heart can make one blue.
The final shape of one's life today lives on only by God's grace.
He or His angel guide when one has more than they can face.

The beauty of one's life can be quickly dashed against the sand.
Today is all there is, so always hold on tightly to it by the hand.
Never, not ever, miss an opportunity to be with one's sweet love.
For it is a blessing to have a dear one on loan from Heaven above.

Elaine Long

MEETING ON THE BEACH

Seagulls were lined up so neatly in rows upon the sand.
They faced the same way just like the members of a band.
This large audience of fowl was led by one lone creature.
A big pelican faced the congregation as if the preacher.

All quietly standing as another gull glides in a vacant place.
Each as if seated on a bench looking into the leader's face.
Their attention all seemed to be united toward just one thing.
As if, they were in flight school class or learning how to sing.

After a long time of sitting still, like they were moving on cue.
Two or three at a time rise and fly from their place on the pew.
It seemed they received clearance and permission to take flight.
One by one, then row by row, their exit was a real unusual sight.

The pelican remained and he had no one left to preach or teach.
A class or church became an empty area again upon the beach.
The congregation had flown up and off upon their way.
The class ended or they didn't like what the big mouth had to say.

WHAT A BEAUTIFUL DAY

It is a beautiful day to behold that the Lord has allowed.
A grand display of puffy clouds makes everyone proud.
The breath taking sunrise that I was blessed to behold.
It creates a memory that I will keep after I am quite old.

The welcome soft breeze kept the temperature just right.
Waves ride the back of the last wave, a wonderful sight.
An unrelenting sun streamed over the sand so bright.
Sunbathers, children and dogs play hard until the night.

Heat lightening in the distance as the day came to an end.
Many meals of shrimp, oysters and clams, we all did depend.
A great sunset could only have been sent from God above.
It was a perfect ending to a beautiful day and filled with love.

Stars appeared one by one only after the day was done.
Drawing to a close such a fantastic day filled with so much fun.
This is magnificent scenery we behold at the beach each day.
It could have only come from God for it is perfect in every way.

Every part of this wonderful breathtaking day was a blessing.
For in the grand beauty everywhere to behold is one big lesson.
May we never be too busy to admire such beauty or not to see.
This exquisite view was really put on this earth for you and me.

Elaine Long

THAT VIEW AND THAT NIGHT

I could only marvel at the magnificent and splendid sight.
The full moon rose from the horizon over the gulf last night.
Only as a blip of light it began the assent and started to glow.
In and through a few clouds its grand beauty started to show.

Really only taking a few minutes until the moon's face was clear.
It was such a majestic moment till one just knew God was near.
The wind of the day now seemed to stop and watch the show.
Witnessing a few minutes of tranquil bliss only few will know.

Never before seeing such beauty as the moon moved in the sky.
Climbing quickly; glimmering across the water as it rose so high.
It was almost like a huge beacon of glow casting its bright light.
Its beam of radiance replaced so much darkness of that night.

Though it didn't, the time briefly seemed to stand still for a while.
In those minutes most troubles could be dismissed with a smile.
We were fortunate to be in a place for the performance to behold.
That view and that night in my mind most likely will not grow old.

It is easy to take the astonishing moon for granted most of time.
Yet the full moon took command over the bay; silent as a mime.
It was a breathtaking, peaceful sight and totally directed by a pro.
Only the master of this universe could have put on such a show.

There is no doubt in my mind that it was directed by God alone.
His beauty in everything accentuates Him on Heaven's throne.
A moon rise is another one of His remarkable gifts for us to see.
I am blessed in the beauty of nature and friends He sends to me.

GULF OR OCEAN OR SEA

The multi colors of a sunrise over the waves of the sea.
It can't be described by the mortal words of you or me.
Hues of every color shimmering against water and the sky,
As though God painted a great picture for just you and I.

Nothing seems to be more relaxing than the fine gulf view.
The early morning with everything that is fresh and new.
The land and sea and sky blend to make a majestic sight.
As if to say God is in His Heaven and everything is alright.

The vast expanse of water be it gulf or ocean or the sea,
Seems to soothe the soul and then sets my thoughts free.
Worries and fears of the mind recede like waves so deep,
Calming nerves and finally allowing a fitful type of sleep.

God made the world with more water than land within.
He knew water had rejuvenating abilities to renew again.
Healing waters touch the inner spirit down deep inside.
Allowing a release of feelings one doesn't always confide.

Elaine Long

A Vacation in Paradise

On several occasions before we have traveled down here.
Every visit had something so special to make the visit dear.
But this trip, everything came together and made it so nice.
I suspect this time, the vacation will compare to paradise.

The right selection of loved ones got it off to the right start.
Then the view, and tranquility and good food add their part.
Some sun and rain and wind help to complete the scene.
The laid back living allows the mind to get clear and clean.

Three days somehow have now mysteriously gone past.
No matter how slow we go, the time this week won't last.
While we soak up the salt air and sun, our time will end.
But before Sunday arrives we are in Heaven until then.

It must be almost Heaven because all my angels are there.
I enjoy their company and for a time lose worries or cares.
It is truly a perfect place to assemble and enjoy it together.
From this fantastic place we have memories to last forever.

We have only a few more days left to enjoy our bit of Heaven.
Then we will part and go back to the real world on day seven.
Nevertheless, I will remember this week as the best to recall.
Your presence here with me to enjoy has simply been a ball.

Yet even to be alone in a perfect place with no one to share it.
This would quickly turn a paradise into just another place to sit.
Thank you for escaping with me once more back to the shore.
For spending quality time with me on an island I just adore.

Once More in Paradise Together

The angry surf is forcefully slapping against the sand.
Perhaps it is mad at the world and all the edges of land.
White caps forming way out on top of the swirling gulf.
All of the churning and rolling waves make it so rough.

Winds are whipping so angrily all along the shore line.
Blowing and fluffing up the sand making the surface fine.
All traces are removed of yesterday's visitor's footprints.
Like memories that stay in the heart without a visible hint.

The rough waters keep splashing and rolling to and fro.
Moving with a mission and having somewhere else to go.
Birds are flying almost sideways against the swirling wind.
Once in a while one can get a glimpse of a big dolphin fin.

Clouds seem to be rushing wildly across a darkening sky.
They only allow the sun to peek in briefly from way up high.
Some rain may eventually blow in on the back of the wind.
Even if it does; it won't be long until the sun shines again.

No matter what scenes the surf or sky may mix on this date.
The view is spectacular and the atmosphere here is great.
We are once more in paradise together with a fantastic team.
It is real and wonderful yet is so good it seems like a dream.

Many other places in this world may out do this island here.
Exotic and famous and expensive places both far and near.
A total joy and love found here with this company and view.
It compares to nothing else I want to go to, be at, or even do.

Thanks to those who come here and let me their loves share.
It is a week of contentment and peace and the stress is rare.
Others might not blend in and time here would not be as neat.
My select group of dear hearts is what truly makes it so sweet.

Elaine Long

HEAVEN IS ALMOST WITHIN REACH

The view of the sand and sea play an important part.
As they come together, it is like a celestial piece of art.
The clear sky and water meet and form a heavenly view.
The warm sun's rays enhance all of the shades of blue.

It is breathtaking and relaxing in the soul at the same time.
A better view of Heaven on earth would be hard to find.
Counting of waves or dolphins soothe and calm the mind.
The lapping waves against the shore are peace so sublime.

It sure is the most peaceful and restful place on earth to be.
Peace is in a comfortable chair enjoying the view of the sea.
As the waves roll in, all of the stress and tension roll away.
It leaves such a calmness and feeling of relaxation all day.

An occasional wisp of wind whistles through the sea oats.
The horizon often dotted with faintly visible fishing boats.
Only add to the restfulness and beauty of the entire scene.
Spend a week at our beach and you will see what I mean.

The sun and sky and sand will mold together before my eyes.
The worries, thoughts and fears are gone away into the skies.
Sights and sounds of the beach put one in a hypnotic state.
This mood only goes away on the day we leave which I hate.

Yet all of the beauty and atmosphere can only but compare.
To the group of friends gathered together when we go there.
The select company makes the picture complete and so fine.
The addition of outsiders who want to come I always decline.

Our group is such a perfect match and compliments the mood.
A value of friendship is priceless and anyone else would be rude.
It is so good to hear the beach girls say, "See you at the beach".
We know it will not be long until Heaven is almost within reach.

SERENITY

With our family of seven returning; the mood was good and fair.
We came back to the sun, wind, sounds, and gulls in the salt air.
The rushing water on the sand creating designs of pretty things.
It seemed like heaven on earth complete with the angel's wings.

We count birds or dolphins and fish in and around the white foam.
It is relaxing there at the shore, we left most of the worries at home.
Looking for shells or capturing the view of the very next sunrise.
Puffy clouds by day and at night stars were diamonds in the skies.

A paradise of serenity and a calming spirit was found there too.
For hours on end listening to the waves and enjoying the view.
A rolling and frothy surf was a magnet reaching out to every soul.
Just to sit there for a month would not even begin to get old.

We were surrounded by family which made our heaven complete.
It really made the time spent an ideal vacation and so very neat.
The love we felt there for the week gave to it the finishing touch.
For all the warmth and feelings and belonging just meant so much.

For those who came that week and made it have a nice warm feel.
To be with them really made the entire week so perfect and ideal.
Maybe it was not the place we had gone to stay but the lovely mix.
Sweet personalities and all the love each one's life in mine depicts.

Though the time ran out too soon and then reality came rushing back.
We discovered the week was over and almost had an anxiety attack.
With sad faces we closed our dream vacation and loaded the last sack.
All that was left of our bit of heaven was return home and unpack.

It was sad leaving the wonderful island just where we found that place.
When we return again, the sweet memories we will again embrace.
It renews an incentive to return soon, often and then again once more.
That thought makes this place more special than it already was before.

How Can We Leave?

The closing minutes of our beach time are slipping by.
It is bringing to an end a week of the sand, sea and sky.
Looking back, where did all the days and nights go?
It almost seems like it was a dream not moving slow.

All the time spent here was good and so relaxing as well.
It seemed to have helped everyone as much as I can tell.
Not having Christmas rush or spending a day at the mall.
Yet our being together as a family meant the most of all.

Counting all of the waves is such a time consuming affair.
It is about as intense as trying to count one's own hair.
The water rushes in fast on the next big surge of waves.
Each one is different as if trying to act up and misbehave.

How can we leave such a breathtaking and beautiful view?
Tears may fall at home without this scene out a window too.
Memories are great but we have to imagine the waves sound.
Replaying this beachscape in panoramic cannot be found.

One thing has also made it quite priceless and forever great.
It was having family to share it with, that made it a special date.
All written on the first page of my book of the bests, you know.
Life is just more fun with my favorites with me wherever I go.

As a part of the family, I will always call each of them my own.
Friends and family are precious because they're angels on loan.
Maybe if we concentrate on coming again very soon and fast.
Instead of a sad leaving, all our memories will much longer last.

THE BLESSINGS OF THE UNIVERSE

The glory of a sunrise is all against a brightly painted sky.
Then the breathtaking beauty of sunset as dusk is nigh.
It is above the great strength of waves cresting in the gulf.
The churning waters below them are so angry and rough.

The immense power is a force of ocean and gulf and sea.
It shows an assortment of scenes that are sure to please.
The loveliness is in a rainbow after the wind and the rain.
That can simply refresh the soul and mind all over again.

The vast size mountains are and all of their rough terrain.
Twinkling stars all stretching for infinity over the plains.
It's against the mystery and radiance of a dark night sky.
It rapidly causes one to catch their breath with a big sigh.

A feeling is felt of hope with a continuous power of love.
The power of all these wonders came from God above.
It creates a calm feeling of peace beginning deep within.
This grandeur is such special gifts from our best friend.

How can anyone not be in awe of the Master to behold?
God is the strength of heart, peace of mind, joy of soul.
For all of the blessings of the universe, Lord Thank you.
Always keep me aware of your love and power in all I do.

HOPEFULLY IN TIME

At long last today I arrived again at the shore.
The rolling tide of waves as relaxing as can be.
The sounds and smells and sights I just adore.
Seeing all yet not believe in God is beyond me.

The salty air seems to simply cleanse one's soul.
A gentle breeze blows some troubles far away.
The view of water and sand is just wealth untold.
Every part comes together as if magic each day.

Refreshing and restoring minds from grief bent.
The troubles and hurts, and worries do recede.
Oh the visit to the ocean was just heaven sent.
This glorious gift of a lovely gulf filled my need.

I guess it was just another part of my grief duty.
I'm so glad I returned to the island once more.
For amid the pain I can still enjoy the rare beauty.
Memories are blended with the view of the shore.

People change or die or life just passes them by.
It's like waves on sand; nothing is or will be forever.
Some feelings cause a tear yet others allow a sigh.
My grief has reduced but my loss of love will never.

The beach trip moved some cobwebs from my mind.
My heart is scarred, but wounds have begun to heal.
I will look ahead to tomorrow and hopefully in time.
I can put grief on the waves and then no longer feel.

MY LEGACY IS THE
VALUE OF MY YEARS

WHEN I AM GONE

When I no longer live on this earth any more.
Then you have a job of which you can't ignore.
Read my instructions they will tell what to do.
I've tried to give some help to get you through.

My life has ended now and it was all it was to be.
Don't grieve for me. My spirit's now been set free.
It's free to be among my loved ones to ever roam.
We will wait up in Heaven for you to come home.

You can remember me by some familiar name.
A nickname or the real one it will say the same.
I loved family and friends more than they knew.
I felt their love to me right back just as much too.

Laugh too; as you remember our many happy times.
All of our fun, holidays, and my attempts at rhyme.
Just some good times being had by one and all.
We had more happy times than sad as I now recall.

My voice will be silent, but in your heart I will live.
I've gone away only because it is God's divine will.
We both know that nothing God ever does is wrong.
Go on your way carrying in your heart a happy song.

One day when your leave time too is drawing near.
I'll be close by so you won't have any worries or fear.
Our family and friends will be just around the bend.
Finally, we will all be gathered back together again.

RECIPE OF A GOOD MARRIAGE

In a good marriage some things you will always find.
It is a bonding of hearts and love of the very best kind.
Some conflict and hard times but it is also much bliss.
Marriage is definitely something you don't want to miss.

An unending acceptance of love is so deeply shared.
It is grown in unselfish devotion so lovingly prepared.
Often it is nourished with trust and a hug and a kiss.
This is the type marriage that most heartache will miss.

This union will forever last and be one of the loving kind.
In all you do, always give it 100% every day in your mind.
In love be so quick to forgive and be quicker to forget too.
Marriage takes work all the time not only if it's brand new.

Ask God to ever be the main part of the love you share.
His blessings will make your harmony beyond compare.
Think first about the other one's feelings and welfare.
Show love and affection each day and in every way care.

Let "I love you" and kisses and hugs be the natural thing.
And you will find with love shown makes your heart sing.
Treat every hour of every day as though it was life's end
Say it, feel it, do it, till the day comes to say, "Bye friend".

And over and over you will wish you could go home again.
You can't know how bad it hurts until it happens and then . . .
Life is too short not to live as much as possible in pure joy.
For a love filled life is something death cannot even destroy.

Elaine Long

One day you will only have memories upon which to relate.
What you do now will make each one of the memories great.
Share every day in each and every part of your life together.
Helping each other and all the storms of life you can weather.

A best friend should be the other half of a marriage you see.
And love can only grow if in that frame of mind you always be.
Let the other half be able to see your love for them in all you do.
Your efforts will be more than doubled when returned to you.

MAGICAL SIMPLICITY

The life of a marriage is a mix of good, bad and up and down.
Some unusual situations but some of the best ones ever found.
It is not ever just a man and a woman to a real marriage make.
It requires more sharing and giving than some are willing to take.

Couples can live for years as man and wife and not ever realize.
How very much they failed to ask the other until one of them dies.
The years of fighting wars of life together does not ever prepare.
For emptiness felt inside when the other one is no longer there.

Others can never understand the degree of loss or sting of pain.
When the realization sinks in and of never holding that love again.
The depth of despair one cannot find words to another explain.
Even the tears don't help though they fall endlessly like the rain.

The magical simplicity of hearts so lovingly entwined and bound.
It is but a brief interlude in one's life with the sweetest love found.
No matter if one hasn't any regrets, yet still so many hurts to bear.
The extent of love isn't known until there is a broken heart to wear.

As silly or stupid as it may sound, this gets truer every single day.
All love isn't spoken and when it can't be felt anymore in any way.
The silence is deafening and arms ache to hold what isn't there.
Days and nights are so lonely and made worse by an empty chair.

Not only does a heart ache endlessly but also the empty arms too.
A touch or kiss taken for granted and hearing or saying I love you.
Confidently knowing both hearts existed and beat for each other.
Not allowing any intrusion of this special unique bond by another.

What I would not give to be in his precious presence once again.
Take me serious or you will grow old alone and wishing my friend.
If a message in this jumble of words can accomplish nothing more.
Never waste a minute by not being with the one you simply adore.

Elaine Long

AN AMAZING JOURNEY

It has truly been an amazing journey down the road of my life.
Both good and bad times came before and after being a wife.
Different events happened on the way that troubled the mind.
By the same token there was much joy too and that was fine.

As I look back over the years that probably made me what I am.
There were many times I felt like I was in front of a broken dam.
Still, my journey has not been any worse than what others had.
Also I have too many blessings and miracles to be angry or sad.

Often I hear, "I don't know how you survived or endured your fate."
I honestly reply, "It wasn't anything I did, my belief in God is great."
He served me strength and hope and faith and courage on my plate.
Also a big serving of patience He gave for all the times I had to wait.

As He gave things, He also took away some panic, fatigue and fear.
Most importantly, He would send someone to hold to and wipe a tear.
Many times situations were hard but faith in God was never in doubt.
Surviving this life while looking toward Heaven is what it is all about.

I was not told why I was chosen to walk this entire journey with Him.
But, oh how glad I was to have had Him close when hope grew dim.
Some heart wrenching emergencies turned into definite blessings.
Other stressful times which became miracles were the best lessons.

Life is truly an amazing journey with so many seemingly dead ends.
My only answer for surviving this trip is the faith I have in my friend.
Without His presence I certainly would have been a real basket case.
At the end of my journey I look forward to thanking Him face to face.

A little piece of jewelry representing a journey of life caught my eye.
Now I wear it as a symbol of the remembrance for the days gone by.
My time of love, determination, and kindness were and are a mission.
All of the reasons come from Him, and for me is a God given position.

DID YOU EVER WONDER?

Did you ever wonder what words will be said of you when you die?
What kind of things could one hear before, or after they might cry?
Some nice and kind points hopefully said would come to the mind.
Sweet words would be wonderful adjectives and of the best kind.

But in a lifetime of all the ups and downs, one simply never knows.
Many times one's words may have hurt or stepped on some toes.
Perhaps a funny thing or act of kindness may be remembered too.
Hopefully good remarks said would be very many and also true.

Though I won't be there to know or probably close enough to hear.
I'd like to think some small thing I did or said helped someone dear.
I wish to be remembered as open minded, flexible and always fair.
Maybe someone felt I had common sense and did always really care.

My word was my bond and it would be done no matter what the cost.
Remind everyone that without their friendship I would have been lost.
One rule I kept that was of the highest importance to me on every day.
I never intentionally hurt feelings or belittled one in person in any way.

Though not to say my temper could flare and hell hath no fury like me.
A difference between telling one off and demeaning character you see.
But if I failed in all of these, I hope to not be recalled as being too rude.
Or to have behaved badly, created problems, or caused a sour mood.

Money does not have enough value to buy life's most important thing.
Only love is the most valuable asset to have or give or to be leaving.
If only one thing my memory can recall to others for years to come.
Let it be said that all my love was unconditional and forever to some.

Elaine Long

AN AWARENESS OF SIMPLE THINGS

To enjoy the finer things in life one must always stop and observe.
See and hear delightful things which would be otherwise unheard.
Blissful enjoyment is time sitting quietly and listening with both ears.
The greatest blessings are usually found in things one softly hears.

A fascinating sight is watching all the birds going about their day.
The light breeze rustling through the many leaves in a gentle way.
Much giddiness of excitement felt in waiting for a special vacation.
The magical anticipation of Christmas day is with childlike elation.

The unusual formations of puffy clouds suspended across the sky.
Those so many wonders of creation are always quietly passing by.
I always try to remain vigilant, hoping for each precious sight to see.
Many of life's ordinary moments hold another lesson and for free.

In our busy rushing world it is certainly easy to not have time to look.
Beauty and awe can be observed when one's time is not over booked.
A new awareness of the simplest things can be taught to the mind.
Yet taking time to enjoy love and life; is time spent of the best kind.

The sights of today and love are what makes tomorrow worthwhile.
For these two things can turn a bad day into one with so much style.
Look for the extraordinary and unusual within the ordinary things.
Things like beauty and laughter and friendship makes a heart sing.

Hunt the rainbow today because tomorrow's cloud may spoil the day.
Never put off enjoying life just because some obstacles fall in the way.
God gave to us the great capacity for love as well as a need for it too.
I would think He would want us to see it and pass it on in all that we do.

Giving 100 % All the Time

I seldom ask for very little in the span of my daily life.
I am self-reliant enough on my own to face most strife.
I never beg or plead of anyone at any time for anything.
My nature prevents me from ever on others to be calling.

Through no fault of my own it seems I was made this way.
I would rather help someone than to be a recipient any day.
To please has always been my aim and desire and the goal.
This is not any different even now when I am growing old.

My philosophy in life has been to give 100% in all I could do.
Still in this process I only take back 10% in everything too.
Then hopefully I could always have and be the true friend.
All of the love between will last through and until life's end.

Yet the hardest part is to allow or receive help from anyone.
The idea of being a problem or a burden is not good or fun.
Many years were helping other's problems and special needs.
It has prevented a leaning on others trait to grow or succeed.

So as I get older and meaner and ornery and so cantankerous.
It is from my independence and not wanting to cause a fuss.
I will try to be good and kind, yet not promising nice or sweet.
But please remember too, for me that is the most difficult feat.

Maybe God put me here for a life of service to others and to all.
I was made by and for His divine plan and daily wait for His call.
God blessed me well though my route has not been trouble free.
Thankfully I will pass on to others in the way He has given to me.

Elaine Long

Did I Make A Difference?

I have now lost most of my family and some of the ones I love so.
My time left on earth is much less than what I have lived I know.
There is always a reason and purpose for everything I believe.
Sometimes life presented me with more than love could relieve.

Did I take full advantage of every chance I had to do some good?
At my life's end will I have done everything that I possibly could?
Was there a heart hurting that I should have listened to or eased?
Could I many more times have found answers from on my knees?

When life's race has been run and my final score card turned in.
Will I have done enough to have helped someone's heart mend?
Or did I say something to cause them more hurt and tear stains?
I will always wonder and hope I did not cause anyone more pain.

I could have had more compassion and visible emotion to show.
Maybe if I had a softer voice and my patience not being near zero.
Whatever attributes I have to use to interact with others each day.
They are from God and assigned to me at least I look at it this way.

I hope I did not lead someone astray or increase their pain or woe.
My intent was good and I loved you more than you will ever know.
No matter the reason or the outcome; my concerns make me say,
Did I make a difference in someone's life even in some small way?

Dear Lord, only you know all of the past and the future still ahead.
Only your plan and your decision dictate what will be done or said.
My constant prayer will be asking you to use me in all I need to do.
In the time I have left here Lord let me to make a difference for you.

No Time or Too Much Time

Not anyone has the promise of another tomorrow.
If a loved one doesn't live for it we are left in sorrow.
A relation to the loved one isn't the biggest concern.
Sometimes it is the unprepared painful way we learn.

An unexpected or tragic death is doubly hard to take.
The flood of grief doesn't allow one any sense to make.
It is impossible to put into words the depth of the despair.
As one is given the news that another is no longer there.

Any chance for last words is lost as well a final goodbye.
One is left with acute shock and grief and endless whys.
This loss is devastating to the core of one's being and soul.
The emotions and memories of that day will not grow old.

Yet there is another type of a death equally as terrible too.
A terminal illness and knowing there is nothing one can do.
The ever present dark cloud of impending doom fills the air.
An inevitable question of how little time left will be there.

There is time, too much in fact for one to say a last goodbye.
It is impossible to say bye for we keep hoping they won't die.
As long as there is any hope we close our minds to reality.
Endless prayers for a healing miracle are a constant plea.

We continue to search for cures or time at any price to buy.
No matter how a loved one dies there aren't any goodbyes.
Could it be this is simply another of God's merciful plans?
We tend to forget God has wisdom and it is all in His hands.

Elaine Long

Maybe a final farewell has not any place in His overall plan.
The one dying will be leaving but bound for Heaven's land.
God is waiting to meet us in glory and to welcome us home.
In a land without goodbyes and we will never have to roam.

I do not have any idea but over the years I find this to be true.
At times there isn't a chance to say bye no matter what we do.
Yet when there is time we can't bring ourselves to say so long.
No time or too much time, we can't say it before they are gone.

I Have No Idea

The wonderful love of God is always so rich and pure.
For an eternity and even for infinity it shall still endure.
It goes far beyond any other realm of love or any care.
For nothing of this world to His love can ever compare.

God had His divine purposes selected for each one of us.
It was before all of mankind was created from some dust.
I am not smart or even very bright or stand straight and tall.
However, God made me for a purpose and that is His call.

I have no idea or explanation for what I was sent here to do.
I try my best to be liked by all and to a few say "I love you".
But at the end of each day to someone I know I have failed.
To another heart I should have been more kind and prevailed.

My mouth should always be closed with only my mind open.
And on that task I'll keep working and will keep on hoping.
My faults are many, so I pray for forgiveness and direction.
God created us like Him, except for His flawless perfection.

Only by faith and His care can I hope to see His plan for me.
I pray my compassion for others will always be easy to see.
It is with great humility I offer my well-worn help for relief.
My strength and hope may waver, but not God or my belief.

JUST HAVING FUN

When I have the idea of something to do for someone.
I do not think of it as a gift but simply of just having fun.
Not even once do I consider it to be any kind of a deed.
But only as thinking of something another might need.

I do not expect to receive the recognition or any praise.
In fact I had rather do it privately or in some quiet ways.
That someone never needs to know from where it came.
Sometimes if it isn't done in secret, it just isn't the same.

In each new day we can decide just what we will do or be.
We are guided or led by our actions and feelings you see.
Every new day is an unblemished gift and yet unmarred.
By another day's end we have left it blessed or all scarred.

Be gentle with yourself every day and especially to all others.
It is about peace of mind and trying to love all of our brothers.
Release your deepest worries and to God all those surrender.
He will take care of all of them and then no longer remember.

Memories of situations or deeds enjoyed we will never lose.
They will be warm reminders from which to pick and choose.
Being kind to others helps feelings and doesn't go out of style.
It also may help someone who is traveling some lonely miles.

I ask God each day to permit me to someone be a blessing.
To do the simple and kind things without any fancy dressing.
Let me have fun and maybe a difference to someone make.
Allow me to be there when one has more than they can take.

PEACE AND QUIET

The growing sound of voices tumbles in from every side.
Rising and falling like the ebb and flow of an ocean's tide.
Each one excitedly telling of the things they have got to say.
One loud voice running over and gets into another's way.

The volume rises and with each one trying hard to be heard.
It makes a noise like a burst of fireworks with each word.
The vibration of sound draws my tension evermore tight.
It raises the level of stress until it is near the insanity height.

Making me wonder just how much more of this I can stand.
Soon the result on my nerves I no longer have command.
Talkers with expressions and dramatics also add to the din.
I sure miss the peace and quiet of home sweet home again.

Maybe I should get some ear plugs to at least help to block.
All of the noisy chatter and my brain would not shake or rock.
I could then decide which soft words I would be able to hear.
So upon my emotions and nerves it would no longer appear.

Then through the endless chattering I could nod and smile.
They would be happy and I could answer just once in a while.
I could again be a human being and not be embarrassed at all.
And not feel like running, screaming and crying down the hall.

The silence would be so golden and quite lovely and sweet.
Not having to pretend to be ok would be once again be neat.
My mind could do the things it so desperately needs to do.
I would not be in a fear mode waiting for clatter to get through.

Elaine Long

It wasn't always so stressful to me to react to loud noise this way.
But now all of the thundering roar can sure ruin the rest of my day.
On top of the pain of loneliness deep inside me makes it so loud.
The strain of that emptiness seems on everything to place a cloud.

Guess the best thing I could do is just disappear and run away.
I would really like to be me and not have an urge to scream or say,
To those near me, "turn your sensitivity up and volume down
Or the next time you look for me I won't be anywhere around."

TAKE NO CREDIT

I have no idea why I was ever sent or left on earth.
My value to anyone by myself is of such little worth.
I have no reason or plan for some things I might do.
The idea comes from out of nowhere and brand new.

When it is a deed or word or thought that I have had.
It is never my doing that might make someone glad.
The dear home I was raised in could have set the tone.
But much compassion or calm came after I was all alone.

I take no credit for anything I may have come to be.
It has never required any of my assistance you see.
I am only a mound of clay and the potter is so great.
The Master is ever in control, and all I need do is wait.

Anything I do or say is never done for praise or show.
I had rather do things quietly so no one will ever know.
The greatest joy is in having sweet loved ones to share.
Enormous wealth comes from feeling their love and care.

Do not feel my act is tough to follow or be your way to do.
Or keep wondering and trying to do or be just like me too.
Don't even worry about trying to fill anyone else's shoes.
It is God's doing and only He always holds all of the clues.

His plan for each one of us was designed before we were.
He has a perfect reason for everything and also the answer.
Each one's purpose has been fulfilled by God's own hand.
It is in His wonderful love and grace that we forever stand.

Elaine Long

THIS LIFETIME OF KNOWLEDGE

I must say my traveling through life has been educational.
Some chapters were bland but the others were sensational.
A country and meager beginning gave my life a realistic start.
Pure common sense was taught as the most important part.

Being poor gave humility and compassion and know how.
Some years of carefree living taught stability then and now.
All of the experiences of stress sure were overly abundant.
Most of all for excitement I never had to look for or to hunt.

I do not regret any errand my excursions have sent or led.
The assortment of education filled up both heart and head.
This lifetime of knowledge made the difference many times.
A simple life of work and God fearing made everyone kind.

An unshakeable trust in God gave calmness I still feel today.
Faith never fails me even now and got me through bad days.
A degree in patience and persistence I earned the hard way.
A role model in care giving that lasted me years not just days.

A full course in friendships short and long helped me every day.
Some good teachers helped to mold my footprints all of the way.
They all had a hand in how I got over mountains I had to climb.
His or her impact gave sense when life had no reason or rhyme.

Memories in cooking, yard and farm chores are scenes I still hold.
Good sense to fix, make do, or devise was an accomplished goal.
Years of working beside a man of many abilities enhanced my traits.
His good judgment and gift of talent made that schooling first rate.

My destiny was chosen probably a long time before I came to be.
All of the reasons and the results will one day be explained by He.
Sometimes life was bright and calm or dark and long, or some test.
Life experiences still ahead will be met with principles from the best.

TOO BUSY TO SEE

Life is at times too hectic to do all I need or could.
Things do not always happen just like they should.
Sometimes I am too busy to be quiet so I can hear.
When God sends his angels to be near and dear.

Too much to do or too tired to see and recognize.
The pain or hurt or grief in someone else's eyes.
Too rushed to see a need or take the time to care.
Not taking the time to listen or compassion share.

Why am I too busy to see one's tears behind a smile?
Am I lost in concentration of something all the while?
Too much of everything is wrong now in this life's race.
So I will take time to talk to God in some quiet place.

Then again I will have time to pause and observe today.
 So I can help to ease someone's trouble along the way.
Then I will be able to hear God give to me His plan to see.
I can hear the sound of angel wings guiding the way for me.

WHEN IT IS GONE

If you could see some things of life through my eyes.
There might be a chance for you to begin to realize.
Life goes on and everything should be normal now.
Yet much changed and won't be the same somehow.

In an instant one's life goes from joy to gut deep dread.
Words cannot describe the agony when a mate is dead.
The loss is unimaginable and yet the life change is unreal.
No more can one fit in or be the same or ever truly heal.

In a world of twos and pairs, being one simply doesn't fit in.
The whole world is geared to twos and couples and in kin.
One alone is an outcast, out of place, very lonely and sad.
Only after a loss can one really realize how much they had.

Look at a pair of gloves, the other is no good if one you lose.
A pair of socks lose one and the other can no longer be used.
Second place or second rate is how the single scene is viewed.
The heavy heart alone only gets bluer with rain or a dark mood.

I guess to lose my mind or just go crazy will not be too far to go.
Alone in the paired world I pray you never have to see or know.
Never miss a chance to share the company with one another.
For when it is gone, one is left all alone in a place like no other.

YOU CAN COUNT ON ME

Don't be concerned about me for I am going to be just fine.
I know you worry some and seem to have me on your mind.
But should my time to go home come without any warning.
Don't grieve if I am not longer on the earth come morning.

Just remember and do not forget how much I love you so.
I always will, no matter where or when it is my time to go.
This is the most important thing for you to feel and know.
Never let this feeling be damaged by any amount of woe.

The sweet memories held are remembrances of our love too.
I certainly enjoyed all the great times I have spent with you.
Life and love and family and friends are not all there ever is.
One's living only can begin when they become a child of His.

There is an amount of time each one of us on earth is allowed
This isn't known before we travel to Heaven beyond the clouds.
Please do not cry or mourn for me or be lonesome or feel sad.
Remember where I am going and only be joyful and real glad.

My trip home on angel's wings will certainly be one of a kind.
So everyday rejoice for me that for all of eternity I will be fine.
Also just inside of the lovely pearly gates I will stop and stand.
There you can count on me to be the first to shake your hand.

When and if my time is drawing near to travel through the sky.
Or if it comes without warning and no time left to say goodbye.
Just know if I am no longer here then I have gone on home.
God sent me for a purpose or reason, but I was only on loan.

Elaine Long

MY ROLE IS LOVE

For quite a few years now I've lived on this earth.
Many times wondering if I had very much worth.
No beauty or any talent or a claim to great fame.
Not anything special about me or even my name.

God is great and always knows what will be best.
I am thankful for much and have been so blessed.
I have a loving family and great friends at my door.
Their presence in my life is always much to adore.

From time to time they can have some small need.
A worry or illness or hurt will make the heart bleed.
Reaching out for help and to me they place the call.
Then it becomes my privilege to give to them my all.

On my own I have no magic or answers or one clue.
But I ask God often to show me what to say and do.
Then a reason for my being here swings out into view.
Now I know exactly what I was put here on earth to do.

The worth or purpose is not wondered about anymore.
My role is love while the many blessings over me pour.
God chose me for the one to polish their angel wings.
They can pursue their concerns and fight other things.

Thank you God, for allowing me to have this special joy.
I have my family and friends close by to love and enjoy.
Granting so much more in return than I ever could give.
I will be thankful for my precious angels as long as I live.

All of the Problems

Your pathway and mine have been different corridors to walk.
So for me to say that I know how you feel would just be all talk.
Yet I do know each situation puts big demands upon the heart.
On some days, one simply does not know how or where to start.

I learned that some questions will not always an answer need.
Or all the problems won't be solved even if we desperately plead.
Not day-by-day, but only hour-by-hour can be met and achieved.
Any peace of mind is welcome and allows a heart to be relieved.

The caregiver is only human and not some kind of a superman.
Do not attempt to try to do everything all the time, for no one can.
To be present at the finish, everyone must pace themselves as well.
I often thought this old caregiver role must have originated in hell.

The continuous weight on the heart will ruin many a night's sleep.
All the frustration, desperation and gloom grip the heart so deep.
An endless weight is on one's shoulders to do and fix everything.
The steady pressure and dread on the mind and heart is crushing.

The relentless stress is intensified by all of the errands and trips.
Often paperwork and insurance on the mind will leave a real grip.
The hours of a day are never enough to get all things completed.
Unceasing demands will only serve to leave one feeling defeated.

I am so aware of the mental fatigue and ever present desperation.
While I cannot fix it, I stand ready to help without any hesitation.
God never puts more on us than we can accomplish or withstand.
His help often comes by sending a good friend to lend us a hand.

Elaine Long

NOTHING ELSE MATTERS

It was a regular day with no idea of the danger soon coming into play.
The precious breath normally taken for granted endless times a day.
Then such an utter feeling of helplessness quickly came to my mind.
Sensing it would not be very long before leaving this world behind.

Many faces and thoughts were racing on my scared and fading mind.
What scene of horror would be left for some others to have to find?
No fear of death, only for the love ones and no time for good bye.
So much left undone and unsaid, suddenly everything had gone awry.

A panic attack is about as useful as something coming out from hell.
It rips out all chances of rational thinking and common sense as well.
Then the heart racing is and lungs aflame all in search of some air.
Yet causing the mind to slow down and begin to not much longer care.

It is not about a little something they call the mind over matter routine.
Only ones who ever struggled to breathe can really know what I mean.
Allergy, or age, or disease doesn't matter, the end result is the same.
To live is to breathe and keep breathing is the only name of the game.

My mind lets me know quickly if there isn't air, it will just not work.
The uncertainty of the next breath can make one soon go berserk.
The saying." nothing else matters," about some difficulty to breathe.
It was said by one in a gasp for air which did not their anxiety relieve.

Panic rages when the abundance of air into the lungs ceases to flow.
Take it from one who found out, the body doesn't have too far to go.
The ingredients of fear and panic and anxiety provide an ugly mess.
It causes a terrifying dilemma which possibly describes it the best.

There may be a more terrorizing sense but I will just take one's word.
My own sensation of smothering left my heart and body so disturbed.
Each breath is precious and one never knows when it could be the last.
Now I don't put anything off till tomorrow or it might not come to past.

A BLESSING OF SWEET CONNECTION

There will always be some things that will bring to mind.
The sharp reality of any life without a love, I must resign.
Those little things couples do without thinking every day.
Serve only as a reminder of a life that a death took away.

Love words with understanding looks or the fleeting smile.
These are some things that make couples lives worthwhile.
These are gentle reminders of the loss of this way of life.
At times it brings a smile, and other times it cuts like a knife.

So many little things some tend to take for granted so much.
Like a special time, or a day, or shared memories and such.
Oh, don't be sad for me or alter or ever omit any of your ways.
Never pass up an opportunity to be with a love or spend a day.

Let every minute create a lasting memory all along the way.
For those precious pictures will be all that is left to hold one day.
Ask all the questions and write down answers and keep it near.
Add to it now and then and if ever required, it will remove fear.

Though if needed, any preparation will never be quite enough.
Walking on alone through life one day will be unbelievably tough.
Do not alter or avoid anything that real loving couples say or do.
For it is a blessing to have a sweet connection among the two.

Love and do with that loved one each day as though it was the last.
For happy years, are like minutes and they slip away so very fast.
Thank God every day for the miracle of having a deep and true love.
A genuine love encircled around the heart, only comes from above.

Additional copies of this book
     are available at:
Bookstore.Authorhouse.com and
Amazon and Google.com and E
books including Kindle, Nook, Sony,
and others. It can also be found at
Barnes & Noble and Books a Million
stores.

God Sends The Words I Only Hold The Pen

CPSIA information can be obtained at www.ICGtesting.com
Printed in the USA
LVOW131311120412

277342LV00001B/5/P